CARL'S STORY:

THE PERSISTENCE OF HOPE

Von C. Petersen

From the author:

All the events in this book are based on true events. Over 20 hours of taped
recordings made by Mr. Willner over a period of 30 years coupled with numerous
conversations with the author were utilized in the creation of the manuscript, and every
attempt was made to provide an accurate depiction of Mr. Willner's experience.
Where needed, certain dialogue and descriptive narratives were utilized to assure
a cohesive element to the book, but nothing was added to the story which had not
actually taken place.
This is a book of non-fiction written in the form of a novel.

ISBN: 978-1-4357-0938-6

Published by Lulu

YOU MAY ORDER YOUR OWN COPY DIRECTLY FROM
THE PUBLISHER AT:
http://stores.lulu.com/voncpetersen

"With everything that's happened to me............
I am still a miracle. I am a miracle man.   When I look out my window to the ocean, there is only one thing I can tell you;
Life itself is a miracle that should never be taken for granted...be grateful for all that you have"

Kalman (Carl) Willner
South Palm Beach, FL
2006

CARL'S STORY:

THE PERSISTENCE OF HOPE

VON CHARLES PETERSEN

CHAPTER ONE

heaven

One spring day across a shadow of time in the not so distant past, a young man had come of age. He lies naked on a bed of moldy straw and covers himself with a tattered blanket. For the first time in six years he prays. The prayer is simple and direct. He asks only that he may die.

"Please God, let me die. Let me die. Please, just let me die."

These were the unspoken words of a soul laid to waste by forces he could no more understand than he could control, yet to which he was inextricably bound. This young man had gone by the name of Kalman Willner before it had been changed to nothing more than a number tattooed across his emaciated arm.

He had come of age within the belly of a beast which had poisoned the world with its dark heart. For six years he had survived incomprehensible horrors. For six years he had languished within the ghettos, work camps, and the death camps of Auschwitz, Dachau and Buchenwald.

Now he wished only to die.

To end the suffering.

The flame of his spirit was the flicker of a candle against a hurricane. It had kept burning for six years, but it could burn no more. As the prayerful words began to die out, muffled between the blanket and straw, a disheveled man burst through the door of the barrack. Running up to the boy laying in the bunk next to Kalman, the man began yelling excitedly. "Hold on brother! Please hold on! They're coming! The Americans are coming. You can hear their guns. Please hold on – they're sure to be here in five or six hours. Just hold on a little longer," he pleaded desperately.

Hearing these words, Kalman - who at nineteen years of age weighed a mere seventy five pounds - a *musselmann* – a man of skin and bones, drifted into the sense of an anesthetic dream.

"Six hours," the young man's voice rang out.

The vibration from the man's throat carried through the air and caught Kalman's eardrums, causing them to quiver. The quivering eardrums transmitted the vibration to his auditory nerve, which carried it into the part of his brain which registered sounds - and sounds into a voice - and a voice into words. Kalman could not register the sound or the voice; he could not have repeated what he had just heard, but deep within his mind, he knew – and he understood. *"They're coming...six hours...."*

He began to count to himself, slowly and deliberately, without thought. "Six years. Six months. Six weeks. Six Days. Six hours…"

Kalman slowly opened his eyes. All was white. The place he now laid was pure white and his skin was cocooned in softness. Surrounding him were white walls and there were what seemed to be nuns walking about the room who were also dressed in white uniforms and habits. Standing next to him was a soldier donning a white jacket, his face tanned and weathered, his features seemingly chiseled in stone. Tears swelled in the soldier's eyes and streamed down his face as he looked down at the living skeleton lying in the bed before him - at Kalman the *musselmann* – and his heart wrenched.

Kalman gazed around the room through the haze of his eyes. Everything seemed to be transparent, the corners of the walls, sharp angles cast in wood and plaster all shimmering slowly as if made from a cloud, and the solidity of the world gave way to the ephemeral of a dream, as sand creeping slowly through an outstretched hand.

For five weeks Kalman had drifted in and out of a coma. Regaining semi-consciousness for brief moments and seeing only whiteness, he felt himself surely to be in heaven. Waking to the whiteness of the world and covered in the soft white comfort of cotton sheets, Kalman was at peace, knowing now that indeed he was in heaven, and he drifted back into a slumber.

A wisp of walnut brown hair fell loosely from beneath the nun's habit. She had perfectly shaped almond eyes which bore the same deep, brown shade as her hair; the eyes accentuated greatly by the light that shone within them. She peered softly at Kalman. "Will he make it doctor?"

For a long time the two stood silently over the young man, who seemed to represent to them all that was good and all that had gone wrong in the world. If he should die - they feared - hope would die as well, and without hope, the world itself would die.

Finally the captain spoke, his voice a deep baritone, yet shaky and fatigued.

"I don't know sister. I don't know."

The room fell silent again. After a few minutes, the captain continued. "When the medics found him in Dachau, he was lying in a pile of corpses next to the crematorium. He was still breathing and his pulse was barely perceptible, but he was alive. God knows how, but he was alive. They pulled him from the carnage and brought him here. All we could do is wait. When he awoke I felt I was looking into the face of a ghost."

"Or perhaps the face of God," the sister replied faintly.

beginnings

When does a person first realize he is alive? What awareness, what sight or sound or feeling marks the beginning of the journey on this twirling blue planet as it races through the emptiness of space? When does the persistence of memory begin to build on each passing moment and become a life lived and remembered?

Kalman Willner's awareness began in 1926 on a cool morning at the age of three as he was being carried to school on his father's shoulders to visit the Rabbi-Teacher, Yoski, in the small village of Dombrowa-Tarnowska in southeast Poland.

The two, father and son, made their way down the dirt road toward the Market Square in the center of town. The sky was pale blue and wisps of high white clouds stretched across the horizon. The square was bordered on each side by the main roads which ran through town, unpaved, dry and dusty, except during the rains when they would turn into long, narrow splotches of mud. The Market Square itself was made of cobblestone which had patches of moss and small opportunistic weeds growing between the cracks. In the center of the square sat three public water pumps. Small shops of all kinds lined the streets: a hardware store and textile shop; a butcher and baker; a tobacco and newspaper shop. Housed between the shops on one side of the Square was the Synagogue while on the other sat the Catholic Church. On Friday, farmers came on horse driven wagons to set up tents in the market, where they would trade their chickens and eggs, cheese and meats in exchange for nails, blankets and other assorted goods from the townspeople.

Kalman's father was a self-educated and self-made man, who, at age thirty-two, was already a successful cattle dealer in the village. He made a striking appearance as he walked down the street; tall and slender with dark hair that shone under the sunlight and a soft mustache which highlighted a face that spoke of wisdom beyond its years. Kalman felt invincible atop his papa's shoulders.

When they arrived at the Chedder, or Hebrew school, Kalman sat on Yoski's lap. Yoski had a long beard and wore a pair of round, wire spectacles. In his hands he held an olive-based tablet with the Hebrew alphabet scrolled across it. On a small table in front of them were raisins, sponge cake, honey cake and a bottle of locally brewed *schlibowitz*, a cross between schnapps and whiskey.

Kalman's father stood nearby, watching proudly as his son pointed out to the Rabbi the letter *alef*, then *gimel* and *tet* and so on. "Three years old and already reading Hebrew," Mr. Willner boasted. After finishing the lesson, the three shared cakes and raisins. Kalman could taste the buttery sweetness of honey as it slid across his palate and the softness of cake as he swallowed joyfully - the simple pleasure of food as it warmed the stomach worth more to a child than all the jewels in the world.

After finishing the cake and raisins, Kalman was given a taste of *schlibowitz* in a small crystal goblet. It was bitter to his tongue and burned as it traveled down his throat, and for 80 years Kalman would remember both the sweetness of honey and the bitterness of whiskey. First memories, as with all memories, are often both bitter and sweet.

guilty pleasures

Three years post-*schlibowitz*, at the ripe old age of six, Kalman sat in a room full of children as they received lessons on Moses' law from the Rabbi's helper. Ever the inquisitive young boy, Kalman's wandering eyes scanned the room when he spotted an open box of candy lying on the bench in front of him. As the other children sat mesmerized, dozing, bored or otherwise preoccupied, Kalman carefully reached over and snatched a few pieces of the irresistible treats out of the box. Just as quickly as he pulled his arm back and clenched the candies in his fist, Kalman felt all eyes in the room falling on him. Afraid to look up for fear of the Rabbi's helper, he sat motionless. The lesson went on uninterrupted. Nothing was said. Finally Kalman raised his head only to find that no one was paying attention to him at all. No one had noticed his clutching hands after all. He quickly slipped the candies in his pant pocket and warily sucked the sticky residue off of his fingers just as the Rabbi's helper began to recite the Ten Words - or Ten Commandants.

"Thou shalt not steal...." rang through the pews. Kalman's stomach sank. The boxes of candy were to be sold for a few *groszy* to help support the school, and now...now he had taken some. If Adam and Eve were sent out of Eden for eating an apple, his little head reasoned, would not the Universe take retribution on him for stealing the bonbons? Already he had broken one law, and the Rabbi had just finished telling the students there were 613 laws altogether. Oh my, to be so guilty at such a young age! Woe is he beset with an overactive conscience.

When the lesson was finished and the boys excused, Kalman ran outside to play with friends. He had all but forgotten about the incident until he arrived home and reached inside his pocket, only to pull out the forbidden candy, squashed and melted onto his hand. Sweet as it was, he didn't lick his fingers this time. Instead, he went to the town pump and washed away the remnants of the candy - washed away the sweet pleasure *and* the guilt. Perhaps God wasn't looking, he hoped. Now he had only to explain the dirty pocket to his mother.

family

Seasons passed under the harsh cloak of winter and the simmering heat of summer and life in the village of Dombrowa went on as it had for centuries. Birds welcomed each coming day, greeting the rising sun with chirps and tweets which resonated through windows of sleeping children and of parents bustling about as they readied for the day. Life in Dombrowa was tough, days filled with hard work and harsh conditions and constant worry over where the next meal would come from. Life was often lived hand-to-mouth, but it was also good. Steeped in tradition, the rhythm of the community had been passed on by generation after generation. Surrounded by family and friends, one never need feel alone, and Kalman was blessed with a large, loving family. His mother had come from an ultra-religious, Hassidic family. Her uncles were Rabbis, judges, lawyers, mohels, and ritual slaughterers; while his father hailed from a more liberal, wealthier family. As was the custom, money and religion often married.

Grandfather Willner had died before Kalman was born and grandmother Willner now lived with Kalman's family, while his mother's parents, Labish and Chana Kohane, lived in the village and ran a small bakery. Kalman's father, being a highly respected man, honest, forthright and intelligent, was often called upon to give advice. He acted as an arbitrator in people's affairs at their own request. When a solution could not be found between two parties, they would come to him to settle their differences.

By the time Kalman was eight years old he found himself the eldest of three siblings; Chiel, who was six, Moshe who was two; and finally the newborn Sarah. Kalman and Chiel were so proud of their baby sister that they would often fight over who was going to push her in the carriage. By the time she was two, however, her little legs were plenty strong enough to carry her anywhere she wanted to go, and Sarah was forever bouncing through the house or down the street singing a song - her big, bright eyes flashing and her curly brown hair bouncing up and down like an enchanted songbird or a whimsical wood sprite.

Including aunts, uncles, cousins and grandparents; the family consisted of 82 people, many of whom lived nearby, and the Willner household was always bustling with activity.

Arising early one cool, crisp, autumn morning, as the air nipped gently at his skin, Kalman gazed at a full moon as it hung in the pre-dawn sky above the hills and farms surrounding Dombrowa. It glowed with an eerie, orange hue, magnified by the haze and dust from the fall harvest, and Kalman's curiosity of the world filled him with wonder and awe.

The harvest festival of *Sukkoth* was taking place and the two older brothers reveled in this celebration of abundance and of the gifts God had bestowed upon them and the village. And of all the gifts they could have, it was their mother who was the greatest gift of all, a beautiful young woman with dark brown hair and eyes that always seemed to sparkle. She worked in the bakery at the Market Square with her parents and was a quiet, devoted mother and wife, infusing the children with a deep love and caring that would forever sustain them.

Life was good.

the split ear

While the elders worked, Kalman's week was filled with long days at school. At the age of nine, he became a "scout", akin to a Boy Scout in America, for the Zionist group *Poalei-Zion*. There were several different organizations in the town, groups of roughly forty men whose primary focus was to return their people back to their homeland. For nearly 3000 years the Israelites had been scattered to the wind. Tumbleweeds with deep roots but no soil to plant them in. Through the *Poalei*, Kalman was introduced to the fervor and passion of the Zionists and he was intrigued by it. When Hershel Goldbladt, the first pioneer from town to join a Kibbutz in the land of milk and honey was set to leave for his pilgrimage, it was young Kalman who was elected to compose a song for Goldbladt's departure. Among all the fanfare and tearful farewells that night, Kalman sang the song he had written for the pioneer. "We will miss you," it went in a mixture of Hebrew and Yiddish. "We will miss you and one day we will meet again in Jerusalem...." Kalman sang out with cheerful exuberance.

He excelled in his studies, while his open, friendly demeanor brought him many friends. Yoski, the teacher of the Jewish school, would not tolerate anything but the best from his students, especially Kalman, and often slapped the hand or pulled up by the ears of anyone whom he felt was not measuring up. Not-withstanding his honey cake and *schlibowitz* from years past, Yoski himself was not always so honey coated. When he became angry his tiny spectacles would fog and his eyeballs seemed to spin in their sunken sockets.

"Mr. Willner," he addressed the young Kalman one morning, the "mister" spoken in a forced, high-pitched tone, as if saying the very words was a struggle of composure and exasperation. "Why have you not completed your lesson?" Not satisfied with the answer, Yoski walked over to Kalman's desk, grabbed him by the ears and pulled him out of the chair.

"Why have you not completed your lesson?!" He asked again, but before Kalman could answer, Yoski dropped him from his tight clutch and slapped him across the ear. This time, however, his hand was stronger than his anger, and the tip of Kalman's ear was split down the middle in an inch long gash.

Kalman ran home after school and cleaned the blood from his head. When his father saw him, he carefully bandaged

Kalman's ear, gently took him by the hand and led him outside. Donning his top hat, black coat and walking cane, Mr. Willner walked passed the Market Square toward the school with his son in tow.

When they arrived at the school, Mr. Willner walked straight up to Yoski, who was still teaching a group of students, and without speaking a word, grabbed him by the beard and slapped him across the face with his hand. Yoski began yelling a prayer, looking up to the heavens, "God help me, God help me, a mad man is killing me.....killing me!" he wailed.

Mr. Willner then calmly put his cane in his other hand, and with his free hand again grabbed Yoski by the beard and slapped him across the face with the other. He then looked Yoski straight in the eyes and said," I don't care if you must discipline the child, but never injure him." With that, he took Kalman by the hand and walked out of the room as Yoski continued ringing his beard nervously and yelling for God to save his life from this wild beast.

Kalman learned early that any adult in the town could beat a child - teachers, parents, uncles, grandparents – it was open game. If you crossed the line, missed a lesson, forgot a prayer - open your hand and wait for the stick. The rod was never spared in the Village of Dombrowa, but never again did Yoski lay his hand on Kalman.

between worlds and a silvery moon

Between the Polish school and the Hebrew school; between mathematics and the Talmud; between cultures – both equally mysterious and layered with hidden meaning, concentration and diligence to one's studies was expected and demanded. Knowledge and learning was of the highest priority in the Willner household. The bookcases were lined with works from Tolstoy to Jack London; from Schopenhauer to Spinoza.

"One who is not poor in mind, can never be truly poor," his father told the boys.

Kalman excelled in his academics, but as with all curious children, it was not in books where he found the richest lessons within the tapestry of his young life. A child's heart lies closest to God, and God speaks to him not through words, but of the world around him, the trees, the back alley where friends gather, the kitchen where warm food is being prepared, the laughter of a playmate or the glint in the eye of a young crush. This was life! This was the playground, the empty slate where memories would be written.

Life was full of mystery, especially within the confines of Dombrowa. Midnight was when the dead would walk from the graveyard to the Synagogue to pray, everyone knew that, and each time Kalman walked past the old burial ground in the woods on the edge of town, he would imagine the procession of departed souls making their nightly pilgrimage to the Synagogue where they would gather inside to read the sacred texts painted on the inner walls. Kalman would pick up his pace, sure to be safely tucked away in bed by midnight so as not to inadvertently meet any of the dear departed himself.

The dead were never far from the living in Dombrowa, nor in lean times the living from the dead. And sometimes, the two would meet, the living and the dead in a space where restless spirits reigned. And so it was, when a rich and prosperous merchant evicted a family of nine onto the streets for being late on their rent. The father of the clan, a skinny man with a large Adams Apple, was frenzied with fear and worry.

"How will we live?! What will become of us? Winter is short to come and will swallow us in its' frigid cold."

He pleaded with the landlord, a sweaty man with a bushy, black beard speckled with hints of gray, and a stomach so round and tight it looked like the Hindenburg was being squeezed out of his pants. He also possessed a bulbous nose and a forehead thick and boney like a Neanderthal's, which always made his silk top hat tilt upwards.

"I can't help you," the landlord answered matter-of-factly. "The law is the law and if you can't pay you must leave." Of course he never mentioned that he had already rented the house to someone else for more money.

But the people of the Dombrowa would not allow the family to go without, so the Rabbi and leaders of the town found a small house for the family to live in and food to eat, but the strain was too much for the father and shortly thereafter he succumbed to worry and passed away, leaving nine fatherless children. Soon afterward, the landlord, who had always felt invincible, became very restless and agitated. Feeling responsible for the skinny father's demise, the landlord took care of the wife and the children, putting them in a house twice the size of the one they had, and promised always to keep them fed and clothed and schooled, but still he became more and more troubled.

A deep sleeper, he now found himself unable to sleep at all. He began to lose weight and his once round face began to look hollowed and sunken. He began to dream of the dead father, and the vision of the deceased father began to appear to him even in the light of day. Soon the ghostly vision of the skinny man became the weight of the world on the landlord, and he felt himself being crushed - crushed by the weight of a ghost.

The family had already forgiven him, but still the visions would not cease. Candles in the landlord's parlor would not stay lit. He heard strange noises at night and could not eat. Finally in a state of near panic, the landlord sought out his Rabbi's help, exasperatedly proclaiming himself the victim of a *dybbuk*. After hearing the man's story, the Rabbi asserted, "We must hold a *din torah*. This is the only way."

When the Day of Judgment arrived, Kalman was with grandfather Kohane, a gentle, soft-spoken man who was greatly respected by the gentiles and Jews alike. A man who walked lightly across the ground so as not to kill the sand beneath his feet, never raising his voice or laying his hands on the children, but rather sitting with them and reading the Torah or sharing a story of his own youth. He held no grudges against any man and walked with the humble air of a servant, slightly stooped at the shoulders and gazing downward as if always in thought; a man of great humility and wisdom.

"Tonight, my dear young Kalman," grandfather spoke with a glint in his eye, "Tonight is a reckoning. All things in this world and the worlds beyond are in balance and balance will always be preserved." Kalman looked at him with great curiosity but did not understand the words his grandfather was sharing with him.

"Now come Kalman," grandfather said as he took him by the hand. "We will witness the *Din Torah*, just as the landlord will bear witness to his deeds. *You see, even a man with everything can still have nothing.* "

The two walked until they reached a small *Hadda*, a room where the congregation met. There were three of four clicks or clans in Dombrowa, each centering on a particular Rabbi, who was exalted as if his words were the words of God. Kalman was fascinated by these gatherings and often smuggled himself into the balcony where he could watch them. Usually there were forty to fifty people gathered around an oblong table covered with a simple tablecloth with loaves of *challa* bread and herring scattered about. The Rabbi would ask for silence and then begin to chant a melody in a deep tone; the sounds flowing hypnotically in an odd mixture of joyous celebration and anguished reverence. The congregation would then join in and produce lyrics to harmonize with the chanting Rabbi; adding words and prayers, pledges and offerings until a new hymn was realized. This hymn would then be put to memory and become part of the clan, their heritage and identity. On this evening, however, the mood was foreboding and somber, more pressing, and more mysterious than ever to Kalman.

After a few prayerful offerings the Rabbi got up and announced; "Now it is time." He was followed first by the rich man, who was visibly nervous and frightened, and then the rest of the clan. Kalman and his grandfather stayed in the background as the procession made its way on the short path to the old graveyard.

Kalman was mesmerized as he watched these devout Hasids walking slowly in single file, all dressed in black pants, black overcoats and black top hats as they made their way toward the cemetery to meet with the unquiet spirit of the dead man.

An old, black iron fence surrounded the graveyard and had been completely covered by prayer shawls. The group proceeded through the gate and walked straight to a fresh grave made apparent by a rectangular outline of dark soil with a small, granite headstone lying at the front of it. The fat landlord was visibly shaking now, his face flushed and small beads of perspiration forming over his forehead. The Rabbi walked right up to the tombstone, and without fanfare, began striking the cold granite stone with his cane.

"Dear friend," he began, still beating the cold stone with his cane. "Listen to me. You must forgive this man. He has repented. He is taking care of your wife and family, and he is deeply sorry for what he has done. Now you must rest and leave this man and this earth in peace. Rest now my friend."

The Rabbi then stepped away from the grave. The cemetery was completely silent save the rustling of dry leaves through a high poplar tree.

"It is done," the Rabbi announced.

Kalman and his grandfather watched silently as the small crowd dispersed and began walking out of the burial ground in single file just as they had walked in. The oversized landlord had lost so much weight that he now looked like a deflated balloon - a shrunken Hindenburg as it were - but even though his jowls were now hanging loosely from his cheeks, his face had a look of relief and serenity, and his previously heavy laden steps had lightened to that of a small child's.

When the last of the crowd had passed, Grandfather Kohane took Kalman by the hand and walked the narrow path back to town. They stopped at a small pond on the way. A crescent moon was reflecting off of the still, dark water.

"Grandfather," Kalman asked. "Are ghosts real?"

"There are some things we cannot know in this world," grandfather Kohane reflected. *"Yet understanding that we cannot know is the first step in understanding."*

"Huh?"

"Look at the pond, Kalman. What do you see?"

"Water."

"And what else?"

"I see the moon....and I can see myself."

"And as you look into the pond and you see your reflection, are you looking at it, or is it looking at you?"

"I don't understand."

"A moon reflected off a pond is still the moon, is it not? They are both real. And if a ripple goes through the water, and the moon disappears off of the lake, is then the moon no longer with us?"

Kalman stood looking into the pond at the silvery moon and his own reflection when Grandfather picked up a pebble and threw it in the water, causing Kalman and the moon to disappear into the wave.

"Grandpa!" Kalman laughed. "Now I'm a ghost!"

"You see, there is no distance between us and what we see and hear and smell, between the trees and the birds and the sky above, the only separation is in our own minds."

"Grandfather," Kalman continued to laugh. "You speak in riddles."

"Perhaps, my dear boy, we are the ghosts," grandpa said with a smile as he patted Kalman on the shoulder.

sabbath and the headless chicken

Sabbath was the most special day of the week, beginning at dusk on Friday as the women of the house lit the Shabbat candles. Once the flames were burning the women would make three sweeping gestures with their arms, pulling the light and smoke from the candle into their bosoms, inviting the warmth and the Spirit into their hearts and homes. They would then cover their eyes and say a prayer after which *challa* bread would be broken with salt. Mr. Willner and grandfather Kohane would then recite *Kiddush*, a prayer over wine sanctifying the day. The bitter week would then fade into memory and this special day would begin; a day of family, serenity, and blessings. On the kitchen counter would lay cheesecake, cinnamon cake, chicken, dumplings and gefilte fish. A feast of the stomach as well as the spirit.

People gathered in the main Synagogue to listen to the *Ruv*, the chief distinguished Rabbi, who was well known in Poland. The *Ruv* stood behind the *amud*, or pulpit, and spoke mainly Yiddish and Hebrew with a bit of broken Polish thrown in. *Menorah* candles illuminated the walls, which were covered with passages of the Torah written in Hebrew. As the honored Rabbi spoke, Kalman would look at the Hebrew letters, and under the flickering light of the candles, they seemed to be moving back and forth on the walls as if the letters themselves were alive. In the middle of the synagogue was the *bimah*, the central pillar where the Torah was read, and to the north of that the Holy Arc with the *Ner Tamid*, or Eternal Light, hanging over it.

The Sabbath was the only truly free day of the week and was a day of family and friends. Following the afternoon meal, the elders lounged beneath a large oak tree while Kalman snuck out into the woods with his sister, Sarah, to carve their initials into a tree. After they finished their handiwork, they walked back out to the edge of the woods and entered a dry wheat field. A flock of crows rose up in front of them, their black, shiny wings flapping wildly and sharp beaks squawking loudly with shrill, piercing shrieks. Sarah was frightened and held onto Kalman's leg tightly for protection. As the crows flew off into the distance and became specks of black atop the rolling hills, pasture, pockets of trees and small brick farm houses, Sarah loosened her grip on her big brother's leg and they continued on toward the Village.

When they reached the Market Square, they saw grandmother Kohane walking steadily down the dusty road with one of the grandchildren holding a box of *cholent*, a dish made of peas and meat that they had picked up at the bakery. On the Sabbath there could be no cooking, so the *cholent* was made at a bakery and placed in a box with each family's name written on it.

"Grandma!" Sarah called out, letting go of Kalman's hand and running gingerly across the square to meet up with grandmother. Kalman followed and the four then walked back home together. Later in the afternoon, there were roughly thirty grandchildren at the house, all running to grandmother for nuts and apples while grandfather sat and listened to their laughter. His heart filled with pride for the children, so full of life and promise and hope.

Sarah rambled effortlessly through the crowd of playful, raucous children as if she was in her own world; her rosy lips and button nose twinkling as she sang playful songs in bits of Polish, Yiddish and Hebrew, while Kalman and Chiel busied themselves with a lost chicken head. Earlier in the week grandmother had gotten a chicken from a *Shokhet*, a trained ritual slaughterer, who butchered in the traditional way known as a *shekhita*, which was designed to make it as quick and painless as possible. Grandmother then performed the *Mitzvah*, the process of preparing the bird as her mother had and her mother's mother and every other mother from the time of Abraham, placing it on a clean slab, covering it with salt, cleaning it again and then repeating the process once again so that it would be kosher, or clean.

"God has given us this gift of food and the chicken has given us its life so we may eat," she told the children as they looked on, but the children weren't the only ones looking on. A feral cat had also gotten wind of the chicken. While grandmother was looking away, the wild puss made its move, clenching onto the fresh pink meat and yanking it off the plate. By the time grandmother turned her attention back to the bird, the, headless foul was flying through the air while in the clutches of the cat's sharp teeth. The cat hit the ground and sprinted off. Grandmother darted after it. The children followed suit, all running across the yard to catch the headless, featherless chicken. The cat was much quicker than the kids, but the naked chicken hanging from its mouth weighed it down, and before the cat could make its move out of the yard and into the clear, grandmother, with her stout little legs, cut in front of it and grabbed it by the tail. The cat let out a screech and the chicken dropped from its clenches. The children were laughing hysterically while grandmother picked up the dead chicken, which was now covered in dirt.

The dilemma now was whether the chicken was still kosher.

So they gathered up the chicken and found a Rabbi who deemed that even if the *Mitzvah* was done over, the chicken would not be fit for consumption. The village was too filthy and a chicken dragged through the muck would not be kosher. They would have to buy a new one.

And so it was.

Later in the afternoon the family ate the dish of *cholent*. The fragrant stew of peas and tender meat had been cooked slowly the day before and lent a hearty meal to the Sabbath. The men took a leisurely walk and shortly after sunset, when three stars were visible in the evening sky, they lit the Havdalah candles which signified the end of Shabbat. The sacred day was nearing its end and the bitter week would soon begin. On the Sabbath especially, life was a gift and a celebration. It had always been so and would always remain so, even if only in a distant dream.

the beast stirs

The seasons came and went and life went on in the Village of Dombrowa as it had for centuries. The first known Jew to settle in Poland dated back to the 10th Century, and the lost peoples of Israel had lived in Polish territories ever since. Migrating from throughout Europe in an attempt to escape persecution, they came as engravers, skilled craftsmen and merchants. Instrumental in expanding commerce and trade in the still undeveloped Poland, some became money-lenders and tax collectors, which made them valuable, and often hated, members of the communtiy. There had always been an uneasy coexistence between the Jews and Poles with very little mingling in society. The Jews, and especially the Hasids, retained their own culture and were greatly resented for it. There were fights at soccer games between the Polish and Jewish youths, name-calling, and always an undercurrent of fear in the air, but it was non-violent for the most part. But in the Third Reich of Germany to the north, the tide was changing, and the ripples began to reach the confines of Dombrowa.

Kalman saw for himself the formless fear turn into a solid reality one afternoon which would be forever etched into his memory. A group of people had gathered in front of his grandparent's small bakery where his mother worked. They were yelling and shouting, "Don't buy from the Jews! Don't buy from the stinking Jews!" Their faces were snarled and twisted; distorted by hatred and ignorance. Kalman stood motionless in the street as he watched the scene unfold, yet the stillness of his body betrayed the violent emotion of anxiety, embarrassment and seething fear which swelled within the pit of his stomach. Many of the faces in the crowd were familiar to him: a farmer they had often bought eggs from, a cattleman who once worked for his father, several peasant women whose children went to the Polish school with Kalman, a postman, a policeman and several merchants. All these faces were recognizable, but they seemed alien now; no longer just familiar faces in a crowd, but a herd of strange animals. A flock of stupidly bleating sheep herded by an unseen shepherd of deceit.

At that moment, Kalman wished himself to be invisible, to become the reflection of a crescent moon on the shimmering surface of a black pond. He looked through the window of the bakery and saw his grandmother busily at work, this strong woman with her wig and big, bright, welcoming eyes. The louder the hoodlums yelled, "Poles buy from Poles; Jews buy from Jews!" The more busily she went about making the pastries and bread, but the Belly of the Beast was beginning to bloat, ready to burst, and soon there would be nowhere to hide.

CHAPTER TWO

blisters

Blisters form after the fact. After the fire has singed the skin
in a flash.
By the time it begins to sting, the flesh has already been
singed.
After the blister, a scar forms.
Sometimes deep. Sometimes barely perceptible.
And so it was when the dragon roared and blew its foul breath
onto Poland.
And in the blink of an eye, day turned into an eternal night.

a gentle heart

Herschl Willner, Kalman's father, grimaced as he lay on the tiny bed covered with a hand-made quilt, his legs pulled tightly against his chest and his hands clutching his stomach. Kalman pained just looking at him, he loved his father so, and it hurt him to see his father in such a state. Many days Kalman had watched his dad suffer from *acid stomach* – burning in the bowels – and Kalman could almost feel it in his own stomach, feel his father's pain. Kalman went into the kitchen and grabbed a hot water bottle, filled it with a pail of water at the town pump, and placed it on the wood stove in the middle of the main room. As he stoked the fire, the dampness in the air began to condense, forming moisture on the walls of the house. It was still early in the morning and Grandmother Willner was asleep on the bed in the corner of the room. The crackling of the burning wood caused her to stir and she looked over to find Kalman busy at work.

"Kalman," she whispered. "What are you busying yourself with? Even the birds are still sleeping." Then she saw the hot water bottle. "Oh, I see."

"Um-hmm," Kalman murmured as he added another log to the fire.

"You're a good boy Kalman. Just like your grandfather. Always concerned with everyone else more than himself, God bless his soul."

Kalman had never met his grandfather. He died before Kalman was born, but he carried his name, Kalman Willner, and grandmother Willner saw her departed husband in young Kalman, in his name and his mannerisms, and as such, always had a special place in her heart for him, often to brother Chiel's chagrin. Kalman could get away with anything with his grandmother. Even their father knew it. He knew never to lay a hand on Kalman with Grandmother Willner around, because if he was to beat the boy then his own mother would surely beat on him. And she could. She was as strong as an ox and everyone knew not to get on her bad side or there would be hell to pay.

Nafali Kamm, the horse dealer, found that out one evening after getting in an argument with the old woman. He started yelling at her while she grabbed a stick and took after him. They struggled for a few moments and both flew down the stairs. Kalman ran into town and told his dad what had happened and they both took a carriage back to the house along with the town doctor. When they arrived home they ran up to the porch where Nafali was sitting.

"How could you do this to an old woman?" Mr. Willner yelled.

"An old woman?" Nafali replied. "That is no woman, it is a beast." He looked up and exposed two big black eyes. "Look what she has done to me."

And just as he said that grandma Willner came out of the house, still yielding the stick.

"And I'll do it again you thieving horse monkey!" she yelled as she started to make her way down the stairs.

Kalman's father stopped her and wrestled the stick from her tight clutch.

"Mama, this man's not worth it. Go inside now, I'll take care of this."

Still undeterred she kept going toward Nafali until Kalman and the doctor escorted her back inside while Mr. Willner taught Nafali a lesson he would not soon forget.

"Father's stomach is burning again grandma," Kalman continued. "He's upset about something. Even mom is worried about him."

"And you, Kalman, you worry too much. Your father is a strong man. He will be OK," and in the next breath, knowing that there would be solacing Kalman, said, "Take the bottle to him Kalman. Go now, the warmth will feel good to him." She knew it would not be the hot water within the flimsy rubber bladder that would make her son feel better, but the care that Kalman had put into it.

She had watched Kalman grow from the time he was born and felt blessed to be with her son and his family. She had immigrated to the United States with her two daughters in 1918, but after one year, she knew she must return to Dombrowa to be with her family.

"This is my home," she would say. "It can be no other way." She would sleep on a small cot in the middle of the room along with the potbelly stove but wouldn't have traded it for the Palace of Versailles, for a life without her family would be as a night without stars.

Kalman's father also had papers to immigrate to the US, but shortly after receiving them, he met his wife to be, and the promise of love took precedent. Never for a moment did he regret his decision.

Kalman stepped quietly into his father's room, careful not to disturb him.

"Papa," he whispered. "Here is your water bottle."

Mr. Willner looked up and smiled, though his face was pale and his cheeks burning red.

"Come Kalman, come sit on the bed with me."

"Kalman approached the bed. Mr. Willner took the hot water bottle and placed it on his stomach.

"Very good Kalman, this feels very good." As his dad spoke those words, Kalman's own stomach felt suddenly lighter.

"Now sit with me," his father said, patting the edge of the bed with his hand. "Sit with your papa."

Kalman sat on the edge of the bed, and his father placed his hand on Kalman's thigh.

"You're growing into a fine young man Kalman. And your brother Chiel too. I want you to know that. You'll go far in this world."

They sat together in silence for a long while when Mr. Willner again spoke. "In this world a human is strong as iron in hard times and weak as a fly in easy ones." He gently squeezed Kalman's thigh. "Be strong my boy. Be strong."

"I will papa. I'll be strong. Now you must rest."

"Yes, I will rest."

Kalman got up to leave the room. When he reached the door, his father called out softly, "Be strong Kalman...but never lose your gentle heart."

passing over

April, 1939

Light rain continued to fall along with a spitting of snow. When the afternoon sun came out, moisture was exhaled from the earth, covering the hillsides and farms with a thin, hazy mist.

The week of Passover was upon the village, and everyone was bustling about in preparation for the festive week. Mr. Willner was arranging a shipment of cattle to Krakow as Mrs. Willner gathered the roast chicken, gefilte fish, apples, nuts, wine, cinnamon and *matzah*, unleavened bread eaten to signify the day their ancestors had fled the pharaoh.

Kalman, as the first born son, was required to fast on the day proceeding Passover. By evening, his stomach was queasy and he was getting a bit lightheaded.

"I feel like a swallowed a shrunken walnut," he told his mother. "No, I think my stomach *is* a shrunken walnut," he added. Kalman had never known such an aching hunger.

The sweet odor of apples and cinnamon simmering on the stove didn't help. His mouth watered just smelling it, and he could almost taste it in the air.

"Here," his mother said as she handed him a cup full of water. "Drink this, it'll keep your belly full until tomorrow."

Kalman took the cup and drank the water in one gulp. Still he wasn't convinced that the water would quell his hunger, but he said nothing and went about his chores.

Kalman fasted for the Angel of Death, not for him exactly, but because this grim reaper of the Old Testament had passed over the houses of the Jewish slaves during the 10th and final plague set upon the Pharaoh in the time of Moses. The 10th and final plague was the death of the first born sons throughout the land. The Hebrew slaves had been forewarned and told to put lamb's blood on their doorways to fend of the Deathly Angel. The Hebrew sons were spared and the slaves set free, and a few thousand years later, Kalman Willner was hungry.

Grandma Willner snuck him raisins. "Here Kalman, I don't think Moses would mind," she told him. "And don't worry about your father – I'll take care of him."

Kalman couldn't find it in himself to eat the raisins, and they became warm and mushy in his pocket just as the forbidden candies had years earlier.

At dawn the next day, the Willner household was in full swing. It was a day of celebration. Normally the family would all go to the main synagogue along with all the others to pray and to listen to the Rabbi speak. However, this day was to be different. With all the children gathered around the table, Mr. Willner told them that everyone was to stay home.

"All the family will come here. Here we will be safe."

He looked over at his wife who was gazing out the window. When she heard her husband's words, she turned around quickly and grabbed the *matzah*. "Come!" she said hurriedly. "Enough of this...we have much to do." She tried in vain to act nonchalant, as if this day was like every other, but she could not conceal the look of worry on her brow.

"Mama," Mr. Willner spoke, "The Jews in Vienna are forced to clean the streets with toothbrushes."

"Toothbrushes?" Sarah giggled. "That's silly."

"Yes, that's silly," Mrs. Willner said as she stroked Sarah's hair softly.

"And there is talk of Dachau, of 'concentration camps'," Mr. Willner continued.

"Concentration camp, what is a concentration camp?" Moshe asked Chiel and Kalman, but his older brothers could not tell him, for they did not know themselves. They could not fathom what a concentration camp was. It was a totally foreign word to them, a word without substance - no meaning to attach to it - but they all knew it was not good, whatever it was.

"A concentration camp?" Chiel asked.

"That's where people go to think really hard," Sarah said matter-of-factly. "My teacher told me I had to con-sen-trate more with my studies. 'Concentrate, Sarah, you must con-sen-trate'."

Then without a care in the world she began singing an old song with her high, girlish voice in a mixture of Hebrew, Yiddish and Polish. The boys started to laugh. "Con–Cen-Trate, Sarah, Con-Cen-Trate," Kalman chided his little sister. The mood in the room lightened with the sounds of the children's laughter and even the parents chuckled softly just as the front door swung open.

Family and friends started filing in. First was grandma and grandpa Kohane. As soon as they stepped through the door Sarah ran to grandmother and gave her a hug. Then she turned to grandpa and wrapped her little arms around his leg, stepped back, and looked at him with smiling eyes, turning from his face to his coat pocket. Grandpa leaned over and slipped his hand in his pocket. "Here my little angel, this is for you," he whispered as he handed her a hard candy. "Now Labish, don't be filling the children with sweets, now is not the time."

"Yes Chana," he answered as he winked at Sarah and the boys.

Kalman and Chiel liked Passover the best of all holidays, it was festive and it often brought gifts, including new socks and perhaps a pair of shoes - which on a cold winter's day would make the difference between warm, wiggly toes and solid, purple grapes attached to burning, numb feet.

Then the Goldmans arrived. Mr. Goldman was a successful shoemaker and Kalman's father's best friend. He had procured the Willner's house for them and had two daughters the same age as Kalman and Chiel.

Then the uncles and aunts came. One uncle who hailed from Berlin was deep into the Kabala. Kalman often teased him and his uncle wouldn't even know he was being teased. He was so deep into the mystical that simple earth bound affairs tended to get lost in the mêlée.

The heaviness of the times began to fade as the day progressed. A day spent with family and friends. Every bit of *Chametz*, or leavened grain, had been removed from the house to signify the expedience to which their ancestral slaves had to leave their homes, and also to remove any puffiness, arrogance or pride within ourselves; for pride, like leavened bread, can rise and cause us to burst.

Four cups of wine were poured to use for blessings throughout the *Seder* – the first being *Kiddush,* the prayer recited before the festive meal was served. A story was told from the *Haggala* of the Exodus out of Egypt from slavery to freedom. Fresh spring vegetables were dipped in salt water to signify the salty tears of the slavery; the spring greens representing rebirth and new beginnings.

Bitter herbs were then eaten as a reminder of the bitterness of slavery, and dinner was then served.

Blessing was said at the end of the meal with the third cup of wine while the fourth was left for the prophet Elijah, who was to herald the coming of the Messiah during Passover. This had always frightened Kalman. Mr. Willner, dressed in a white robe would say the fiery blessing with such intensity, such fierce belief, that he seemed surely to be the one to open the door through which the old prophet would pass into our world - right into *Kalman's* house. And sure enough, after the blessing, his father would open the front door in order to invite Elijah into the house. Kalman would sit mesmerized at the table. The wine would begin to quiver and ripple within the glass when the door was opened, and Kalman was certain that old Elijah was there partaking in the wine. Chiel was a bit more skeptical and said it was the wind blowing through the door, but Kalman wasn't so sure, for every year, even when there was no wind, the wine would still ripple.

To dampen his fear of Elijah, Kalman went about finishing the *charoset*, a mixture of the nuts, apples, cinnamon and wine which had made his mouth water as it cooked the day before. Traditionally it was eaten to symbolize the mortar used by their enslaved ancestors to make bricks. For Kalman it was just a little slice of heaven, the best part of the meal eaten with a dab of horseradish to top it off.

What Kalman did not know, but the elders were well aware of, was that traditionally, the door was opened not only as a gesture inviting Elijah into the house, but also done historically to "open the door" for the gentiles, that they may see the worshippers weren't doing anything sinister or forbidden behind closed doors.

This came about after a peasant uprising of rape and murder when the Jews were accused of kidnapping a gentile child and using his blood to make *matzah*.

Fee-fi-fo-fum!

This Passover was to be different, however. After the dinner blessing, the fourth cup sat on the table as it always had, but the front door remained closed. Mrs. Willner began gathering the dishes from the table while the other adults murmured quietly amongst themselves. It was still early in the evening, but there was to be no songs sung, no sharing of stories after dinner until late at night, no walks around the village. Instead, the lights were dimmed and all the guests and family said their good-byes and quietly filed out the door. The house which moments before had been bustling with talk and laughter now stood still, and within the silence, only the fearful beating of one's own heart could be heard.

Kalman and the others retired to bed, and as he lie listening to wind whistling through the windows, he knew Elijah was not coming on this evening – and certainly not the Messiah.

safety in love

Spring gave way to summer's hot, humid days and cool nights. The seasons changed but not Kalman's routine. Wake up at 6:00 to pray, then off to the Polish school with its filthy bathrooms which Kalman refused to use. When he was younger he would sometimes go home with wet pants, preferring that to the stench and waste of the school's restroom. Even the flies stayed away. The teachers, who had no right to be teachers, taught by intimidation, reducing a love of learning to a fear of the paddle. Then he would go to the Hebrew school which was smaller but much cleaner. At night he would visit the Hasidic rooms to listen to the melodies or go out to meet with friends and finish the evening studying and doing his chores. He and his brother Chiel also started working on some small farms around Dombrowa for extra food for the family, for rations of grain, meats and produce were becoming scarce.

Toward the end of August rumors stirred that a German attack on Poland was imminent. Word came to the Willner household one evening under a harvest moon which hung bright orange over the fields and villages.

"All soldiers are to report immediately for duty," the messenger had told them, and before any questions could be asked, he was gone.

Mr. Willner was a decorated hero from WWI, capturing 39 Bolsheviks and receiving the highest medal of honor awarded by Poland. He was Jewish, but he was also Polish, and it was his duty to protect the land just as much as any other citizen. Without hesitancy, he gathered a few things, donned his old uniform with the cross displayed proudly on his chest, and the next morning, he was gone.

Never had Kalman felt such emptiness. The family had never been separated before, and his father's absence left a great void. Kalman wandered through the small house, confused and frightened. He stepped into his father's room and the hot water bottle was lying on top of the bed where his dad had left it. Kalman knew his father was in great pain. Now he was gone and Kalman couldn't help him.

The day passed slowly. Sarah and Moshe thought their father had gone away to take of business as he often did. Kalman and Chiel knew better, but said nothing. There was no use in scaring the children, although they were only children themselves, as Kalman was 14 and Chiel 13. Grandma Willner was angry. "How can such a thing happen in the 20th Century? How can they take a sick man for another war? Isn't one enough? Isn't one too much!"

His mother's parents also stopped by to see the family. Chana had brought fresh food for the family while grandpa cheered the kids up just by being there. His presence was always calming to everyone around him. When Labish Kohane was around, everything just seemed as though it would work out for the best, one way or another. Even though he worried greatly for his son-in-law, he never lost the smile in his eyes or his care for others.

After everyone had cleared out of the house, the young ones were tucked into bed, after which the two older brothers and Mrs. Willner retired. Kalman lie in bed for what seemed an eternity, unable to sleep as his mind spun with twisted thoughts. Everything was changing so rapidly. The world no longer was what it had been, and the future was even more uncertain. Finally he drifted into a slumber, but even in sleep he could not find peace from his troubled thoughts.

Early the next morning he heard his father's voice. He turned over in bed and put a pillow over his head. Surely he had been dreaming and the sound of his dad's voice made him so sad he just wanted to drown it out. Then he heard it again. He opened his eyes and slowly turned over. Standing over him was his dad.

"Sshhh," Mr. Willner whispered. "We mustn't wake the others."

Kalman jumped out of bed and hugged his father as tightly as he could. He wanted to hold him forever and never let him go.

The sound of the squeaking bed as Kalman hopped out to greet his father woke up grandmother Willner. She gasped with relief when she saw her son, and her gasp in turn woke up the others. The children ran into the room and laughed joyously as they jumped on his lap. All the commotion woke up Mrs. Willner. She stepped out of her bedroom and into the main room. Her eyes locked onto her husband's from across the room above all the laughter and noise, and tears streamed down her cheeks. Mr. Willner had indeed checked into the army, but was so sick that he was sent back.

Now the family was together again and that's all that mattered. The world could collapse and the heavens fall, but if the family was together all could be endured. There would be safety in their love for one another. Their care would be the cocoon which would protect them. This was the children's belief and the elder's hopes, but they knew that even a tightly woven cocoon could not protect the caterpillar from the birds of prey forever.

Mrs. Willner understood that there were no safe harbors in Poland, and when the children had all left the house she held onto her husband with all the love of her soul and strength of her arms. As they held each other, Mrs. Willner whispered into her husband's ear. "You must leave Herschl. You must leave Poland. Schindler and Weinberger were here yesterday and they have decided to seek refuge in Russia."

"I cannot Rachel. I cannot..." he began to say, but before he could finish Mrs. Willner cut him off. "You must leave. You will die if you stay. No man will be safe here. They will spare the women and children, but they will kill you. Go to Russia with the others and find a safe place and then we will meet you there."

Reluctantly, he agreed. That evening, he told the children he would leaving for awhile, but that he would return to get them and not to worry. The next day he left with a group of thirty to forty others. For a day and night they walked without stopping. Each step grew heavier, not with fatigue, but with concern for his family. Each step tore at Herschl Willner's heart as he felt himself growing further and further away from his family. Finally, he could take it no more. He must return. Again he walked through the farms and hills and villages without rest until he reached Dombrowa. When he arrived home to the joy of the children, he swore that he would never leave them again. A family must be together and he must be there to protect them. It could be no other way.

war

On the very next day, September 1st, 1939, war broke out. Germany invaded Poland like a thunderous monster. The Polish Army, ill-equipped, tried in vain to repel the hoard, but to no avail. Calvary on horseback raced to the front, but was no match for the mechanized beast that arose from the Rhineland, the strongest army ever to be assembled in the history of mankind.

In twelve short days it had reached Dombrowa.

The Panzers moved in like a plague of destruction cast in iron and fired in hell. Unstoppable, faceless machines. Visions from a nightmare. The air was thick with exhaust. The gritty, black haze hung in the village and farms and burnt the eyes and stung the skin with its filmy residue. So heavy was the burnt fuel that one could not even see across the street through the billowy smoke. The tanks roared through Main Street like a herd of wild elephants on an ant path, shaking the houses as they passed. Sarah sat in the corner on a bed holding tightly to a toy that Kalman and Chiel had made for her. Mr. and Mrs. Willner stood by the window with a vanquished expression on their faces, while the three boys stayed tucked away in the kitchen.

It had begun.

CHAPTER 3

ghosts

S carcely before the smoke had settled, the tanks were gone. Only the lingering odor of diesel and the settling dust on the houses and cobblestone market spoke of them being there at all. That and the tracks, the deep, ridged tracks running down Main Street which seemed to the villagers to come from nowhere and lead to nowhere, yet to extend forever. And they knew, deep within their hearts and their darkest fears, that the tracks were as an umbilical cord which led to the Beast, the beast from which the tanks fed and their small world was now attached.

Everyone stayed in their houses until sundown when the people of the village began to stir under the blanket of darkness. This day had been long feared with great trepidation, but until it had actually come, it remained distant and removed from their lives, like a silent illness that slowly sickens the body but remains hidden from view. Kalman and Chiel ventured outdoors and met up with one of his best friends, Shiek Schindler, whose father was a grain dealer in Dombrowa. The streets were dark except for a few kerosene lamps burning in the windows. The sky was black as obsidian, and the stars seemed to reach down and touch the ground. They walked down Main Street passed the synagogue and made their way to the edge of the old cemetery. Kalman thought of the *Din Torah* held for the rich landlord and restless spirit of the deceased father.

"All things are in balance," his grandfather had told him.

Still, Kalman wondered. How could that be? What were the tanks balancing? And what would balance them? The night was getting late and the boys started back home. Kalman just wanted to be back in his own bed. As they approached the Market Square, Kalman looked back and in the corner of his eye, he could have sworn he saw a procession of old Rabbis making their way out of the cemetery toward the Synagogue.

"Ghosts," he said to himself out loud.

"What?" Shiek asked.

"Spirits," Kalman answered. "Spirits. Do you believe in spirits? In ghosts?"

"You've lost it," Shiek told him. "Anyway, I have to get home. The only ghosts around here are us. We're gonna be the ghosts – all of us," he said as he turned down another path and walked away toward his own home.

The two brothers continued on their way. "Do you think we'll be ghosts?" Chiel asked his older brother.

"No one gets off this planet alive – that's what grandpa said – but it'll be a long time before we're ghosts," Kalman assured

41

him. "Nobody's going to make us ghosts."

When they arrived home, the boys found their mother and father anxiously awaiting them. "Where have you boys been?" his mother asked.

"You must be very careful," Mr. Willner told them, his voiced strained. "You mustn't let anyone see you. Do you understand me? You cannot run around the town without a reason!"

Kalman looked over at Grandmother Willner who was already lying in bed. She looked at him and tried to smile. Sarah was tucked in with Moshe. Finally, Kalman undressed and crawled into bed.

latkes

The following morning, Kalman and Chiel rose at the crack of dawn, said their prayers, got dressed, and made their way to the farm where they had been working since summer. The farmer had been paying them with potatoes for their labor. What the family didn't eat, they stored in their cellar, but the farmer was stingy and the cellar scarcely had enough potatoes for the rats, let alone a family of six, so the boys decided to up the ante a bit.

After the boys finished slopping the pigs and feeding the cows, they went about picking the potatoes. The farmer retired for some afternoon vodka, but before he did, he yelled out at the boys that there were some extra potatoes in the barn. "Help yourself to whatever's in there," he laughed. When the boys went into the barn for the potatoes, all they found was a pile of rotten spuds from the previous season lying in the corner, shrunken like oversized raisins and covered with a black film. "What a schmuck!" the boys murmured. But what could they do? They had to eat.

When the day's work was done, the farmer came back out to check their progress and give them a small sack of potatoes as payment. "Before you leave don't forget to feed the cows," he ordered. As Kalman fed the cows, Chiel snuck out into the woods next to the potato cellar. Once Chiel was positioned, Kalman kicked a cow, which sent the whole herd mooing and stamping about with a loud uproar.

"What's going on out here?!" the farmer screamed.

When he entered the corral to check on the cows, Kalman slipped out the other gate and went over to the cellar. He started grabbing potatoes as fast as he could and threw them out into the woods for Chiel to pick up. Then before the cows settled down too much, he went back and helped the farmer calm them down and gather them up.

"You're done now," the farmer announced. "Go home now boy!"

Kalman left the half-drunken peasant and met his brother in the woods where they gathered up the potatoes in an old burlap sack and carried them home. That evening Mrs. Willner made *latkes* with a scoop of butter and dab of sour cream and applesauce. Food was getting scarce and never before had potato pancakes tasted so good.

hounds from hell

On the very next day, the town awoke to the sound of a jeep and large truck which carried a small garrison of regular German infantry. The soldiers filed out into the street wearing stone-gray uniforms with black leather belts and black hobnailed marching boots. On their heads were Stahlhelms, the familiar steel helmets that looked like coal-scuttles; decorated on one side with a silver-gray eagle and a black, white and red shield; and on the other, a Swastika, the ancient symbol used in cultures throughout time; sacred to the Hindi and Buddhists - now bastardized into a symbol of hatred and brutality.

Each soldier carried a rifle or machine-gun, and the deep steely blue of the barrels seemed to cut sunshine itself in half. Yelling loudly and barking orders, which in the confusion, no one standing by could understand, they pushed through the crowds, knocking down anyone in their way; men, women, children, the elderly, even small dogs. They immediately seized the courthouse to be used as their headquarters, along with the post office, Synagogue, and various other buildings. Many of the Hasidic Jews had never even seen a rifle before. Their belief had always been "to turn the other cheek."

As for the others, unarmed and overcome with shock, disbelief and fear, thoughts of resistance were unimaginable. One soldier with one gun could kill a hundred people in seconds, and behind that soldier were a million others. Although forceful and hard, that first day was relatively free of violence.

On the second day something deeply sinister entered the village. Again a truck and jeep came into town, but this time it was the SS – the Gestapo.

Life in Dombrowa would change forever

The men of the SS descended upon the village like hounds

from hell.

They immediately gathered the mayor, the chief of police, the two remaining Jewish lawyers, the chief Rabbi, as well as thirty or so of the remaining intelligentsia of the town. Kalman watched as they pulled the chief Rabbi from the Synagogue. The SS, distinguishable by the collars on their uniforms piped in black and silver braiding, drug this highly respected man - learned and wise - like a meaningless hunk of flesh through the streets. These ignorant soldiers, who couldn't have distinguished an opera from a minstrel show or a book from a brick, paraded through the street like a pack of wild hyenas, empowered only by their capacity to be cruel.

They drug the chief Rabbi to a large tree where Kalman and Chiel once argued over who would push Sarah in the stroller. Kalman looked on at the horrible scene unfolding in front of the tree, the same tree which once held such happy memories, and was overcome with despair. This is what civilization had wrought upon the supposedly backward world of Dombrowa.

After the soldiers had gathered the group of unfortunate souls, they herded them into the Market Square. In the meantime, the other soldiers began pulling people out of their houses and off the streets and forced them to the Square. Only those who had hidden would be spared the horrific scene that followed. Kalman and his family were not so fortunate.

Under an overcast sky, Kalman stood in the middle of the gathered crowd, along with his parents, grandparents, brothers Moshe and Chiel and sister Sarah. No one spoke. Some of the people were seemingly in shock, while others were near tears, trembling and frightened. Looking through the crowd, Kalman saw what appeared to be an officer. He wore a peaked cap with the SS Eagle and Swastika on the crown and a metal "death head's" on the black velvet cap band. Peering at the death's head, a metallic skull, Kalman was filled with a mixture of disbelief and hopelessness. As he stared at the officer, he felt as though he was looking at a demon standing in the middle of their town, a demon covered with human skin and wearing the uniform of madness.

The officer began yelling something, but Kalman did not speak German and could not understand the words coming from this demon's mouth. Kalman glanced at the people standing in the square, men he had known since childhood, men he had respected and looked up to, and he could see the fear in their faces. The German officer yelled one last time, a short, curt order. A line of soldiers then drew back their weapons and began firing into the men. They crumpled like rag dolls, some falling backwards from the force of the bullets and others dropping from where they stood like marionettes whose strings had been cut. Instinctively Kalman covered Sarah's eyes while Moshe buried his head in his father's side. The compression from the gunfire ricocheted through the crowd, and Kalman could feel the force of the shot on his chest even though he was on the other side of the Square.

Blood spilled out from the crumpled bodies onto the Cobblestone Square, some which were still writhing on the ground, some twitching, but most as silent and still as stone. Where chickens and vegetables and the clip clop of farmer's horses once fell during Saturday market, the heavy blood congealed like thickened molasses and formed dark red clumps between the cracks. The smell of blood filled the air with a sickly sweet odor, which when mixed with the fumes of gunpowder, burnt the nostrils with an odor that no man, woman or child should ever have to endure.

Children began to cry, but were quickly quieted by their parents so as not to draw attention to themselves. The German officer then began to speak again, this time in perfect Polish. "This is a lesson to you all. You are now under control of our Führer and the Reich. All property, business, and people of this land are now ours. Any resistance will be severely punished...by death! Any Jews caught within two kilometers outside of the village will be executed. Anyone being caught giving food or shelter to a Jew will be executed. Anyone found conspiring against the will of the Reich in any manner will be shot. Do you understand?"

After he finished speaking, the officer took a deep breath, puffed up his chest, the corners of his mouth turning up into a barely noticeable, but hideous grin, like that of a sociopathic child after killing a dog. He was *enjoying it*, and this made the unreal scene even more unfathomable to the teenage Kalman. His stomach burned with fear and anger and the site of the executed men lying in the square made him sick. But most of all, he was afraid for his family, and knowing he could do nothing to protect them, felt ashamed and deeply disturbed. As if one fourteen year old boy could stop the German Army.

After the officer had finished his speech, he released the captive crowd and everyone started slowly back to their homes. People's heads hung low, and as they walked down the street it looked like a funeral procession, except for one difference, it appeared as though they were going to *their own* funerals. Mrs. Willner held Moshe and Sarah by the hand, Chiel stood behind his father and Kalman was in the back with his grandparents.

His father was slowly shaking his head back and forth, as if he were arguing with himself, and then Kalman heard him say, "It is God's punishment for our sins. Hitler must be sent by God to punish our sins, how else could he be so powerful?" he asked himself, exasperated, unable to grasp what had happened. They continued walking when grandfather, in his soft and quiet voice, said to Kalman. "This is not God's doing. This is man's."

As they approached their small house, Kalman glanced at the neighborhood, the neighborhood he had known all his life, and even though everything stood as it always had; each tree, shrub, every store and house were as they always had been, nothing seemed the same. The world he had known had disappeared on that day as the shots rang out, and the world became unfamiliar, hostile, and dangerous.

the gentlest spirit

Grandpa Labish Kohane walked down the road as he had for years, his feet stepping softly onto the ground, his head turned slightly down, lost in thoughts of man, God and family; of gratitude and humility. A gentle man with a kind heart. He was making his way to the bakery, which was confiscated by the Gestapo and turned over to a German-Pole who retained the former owners as workers, giving them anything he thought they deserved for compensation. Grandpa had saved a small jar of honey for the children and wanted to get *challa* bread to go with it.

As he ambled down the street, he ran into a group of German soldiers who were yelling and laughing at a family as they walked by, making fun of their strange clothes, the woman's wig, and the children's shoes. Grandpa continued walking until he was next to the soldiers. He strolled steadily and softly, neither slowing down nor speeding up, but maintaining his easy pace. As he passed the soldiers, one of them yelled, "And look at this old fool, what does he think he's doing?" The soldier, a young man, no older than twenty, with a reddish face and sandy hair that looked like coarse straw under his helmet, along with dull, blue eyes, jumped in front of grandpa and knocked the Talmud out of his hands. "What are you reading old man?"

Grandpa looked up at him and said nothing.

"What, you're too good to answer me?" the soldier continued. Then he knocked grandpa's hat off.

Then he grabbed grandpa's beard. "And what's this? This dirty, disgusting beard. It has lice for sure!"

Grandpa tried to pull away but the other soldiers stopped him and held him by the arms. Then they started pulling at his beard, ripping at it like animals, all the time laughing and taking pictures for their "scrap book". You could hear the rip of the beard from across the street, and when they were done they released the old man and he collapsed onto the street. Clumps of hair and skin and blood hung from his face. The soldiers took one last picture and then left grandpa lying in the street.

Some friends of the family had witnessed the whole scene, and once the soldiers had left, ran over to where grandpa lie. He was lying semi-prone, half way between his side and stomach, his face to the ground, with his legs pulled up and one arm stretched out over his head. One of the friends knelt beside grandpa while the other ran to the Willner household to tell them what had happened. The man touched grandpa's shoulder gently, which made him pull away as if trying to protect himself. "Labish, it is I, your friend, you are safe now, the hoodlums are gone." Then he slowly cupped grandpa's head in his hand and turned him over. His face was covered with dirt, which had stuck to the blood and skin. Grandpa's eyes, which had always twinkled, appeared dull and cloudy. He tried to speak, but could not.

Meanwhile, others who knew the family ran to the bakery where Chana, his wife, was still working, and told her that Labish and been attacked. Chana dropped the dough she was kneading, fell to the floor and began to wail in a deep, sorrowful tone, repeating over and over, "God in heaven, God in heaven!"

When news reached the Willner household, the whole family immediately ran into town. Fed by adrenaline, fear and fury, Kalman ran without stopping until he reached his grandfather. Grandfather Kohane was sitting in a slumped position and supported by the friend when Kalman arrived. The vision of his grandfather; this loving, kind man, sitting on the street, his clothes torn and his face brutalized, struck Kalman like a bolt of dark, cold lightening. He was now living in hell, he was sure of that, and to see his grandfather suffer so had verified it.

When Mr. Willner and the others arrived, Kalman took Grandpa by one arm and his father took the other and together they helped him off the ground. Kalman was struck by how light and frail his grandpa seemed. He could barely walk, and often his feet dragged the ground, but with the help of others, they finally got him home, back to the small, unassuming shack he had lived in for many years.

Some of Kalman's uncles went to the bakery to get grandmother Kohane. She was no longer crying and seemed to have run out of tears. She looked straight ahead with a far away glassy stare. The shock had been too much for her to bear, and she was beyond solace.

They lay grandfather onto the bed under the dim light of a kerosene lamp. The family stayed close to him and Kalman never left his side. He became weaker and weaker throughout the night, but it wasn't his physical injuries that seemed to affect him as much as a deep, profound sadness that had overcome him. Near morning, just before the birds began to sing in the fields, grandpa called out to Kalman in a weak, raspy voice.

"Kalman, my child," he began.

"Yes grandfather.'

"Kalman, listen to me, hear my words and do not forget. Someone *must* survive to tell this story...to tell others what is happening."

"Yes grandfather," Kalman answered as tears streamed down his face.

"Yes grandfather."

Then Labish Kohane became very still. His head sunk back and his chin turned softly down into the pillow.

He was gone.

CHAPTER 4

the only hope

The night grandfather Kohane died, Kalman was left with deep sadness and a profound sense of loss. Nothing made sense. His heart ached. His stomach burned. Streams of thought and emotion raced through his mind as he watched his grandfather slip away.

-*Must survive. Life is survival – survival is life! Can't win – they can't win. Hold on. Hold on 'til it's gone – 'til it's over and they're gone. Hold on – one more day. Must hold on. Grandfather! Don't go away! Don't go away and leave us! Please grandfather!*

But slip away he did.

After the gentle old man had spoken his last words and exhaled his last breath, his body became still and lifeless and something within Kalman changed. How or why such cruelty and evil could exist may ride the undercurrent of his consciousness, but more pressing still was the immediate concern of staying alive. And nothing would bring his grandfather back. Nothing.

Kalman gazed around the bedroom. His mother and father were there along with Chiel, Moshe, Sarah, the cousins, and grandmother Kohane. Sarah could not understand why everyone was crying.

"Grandpa is sleeping," she said. "He is right there mama. In bed. Don't you see! He hasn't gone away. He is right there."

Grandmother sobbed.

Kalman looked at the body lying in the bed. The skin was gray and waxy. Yet it looked peaceful. In death he could be hurt no more.

The family was able to say *kadish* and give grandfather a proper burial. As they covered him in a shroud and laid him to rest, Kalman remembered their visit to the pond; the rippling waves and the moon - of what was real and what was not. Reality now was a matter of survival, that much was certain. Every day more and more people disappeared, mainly the old and infirm, plus anyone seen as a threat to the Nazis. Shots rang out across the village and countryside and the bodies were left for the families or the crows, whichever came first. No place was safe. Not in your home, not under the covers; nor in the outhouse and especially not walking on the street. At any time in any place one could be stopped, beaten, shot or hung. Young girls and older women were not safe and this tore at fathers' and husbands' hearts. Burning with rage, many were killed trying to protect their wives and daughters. No one was safe.

A few days after the funeral, grandmother Kohane disappeared and was never seen again. In normal times the whole village would be looking for her. But now, where would they look? And what would they do if they found her? And who *could* look? Every family was losing members. And no one knew who would be next. Every day was a matter of survival. If you could survive one more day, perhaps it would end. That was the hope. The only hope. Surely in time the world would come to their aid and put an end to the madness. That was the hope. Just make it through one more day.

red apples

Ten days had passed since the arrival of the Germans in Dombrowa. Grandfather Kohane and his wife Chana Beila were gone. Mr. Weinberger, the lawyer who had fled to Russia with Kalman's father, had returned and was made head of the Jewish Council, a body the Nazi's had set up to act as liaisons between themselves and the populace. The council was responsible for ensuring all the laws and demands set forth by the Reich were understood and followed. A group of about 20 men were picked as the Jewish police force, mainly a bunch of lecherous pigs with big sticks, men who previously felt powerless and now had a chance to even the score with those they envied. A law was passed stating that each family must provide one person to work for the Germans, and each day they demanded a certain number of workers. On one occasion it may be ten, on another it could be a hundred. It was the council's responsibility to find the workers. Sometimes the soldiers would demand money or workers.

"You will find 100 able men to work for us or you must gather a sum of 10,000 zloty," the hawk faced officer with the death skull would demand. "If you fail to do so by sunrise tomorrow morning, fifty people will be shot."

And so it went. The workers, boys and men and even women and girls would spend sunrise to sundown doing whatever the Germans needed done. Digging trenches, gathering food from farms, carrying materials, all the time being screamed at, spit on and tormented by the guards. They would return home exhausted and hungry only to find what little supplies they had left had been taken by other soldiers. Luckily the Willners had a small stockpile of potatoes left over from Kalman and Chiel's farm work, but it was hardly enough for bare sustenance.

On the tenth day of occupation came Yom Kippur, the highest of Holy Days, a time of atonement for one's sins, a day "when even the wind and rain knew it was coming. It was a time of forgiveness and of who would die the next year: Who would die by fire, who would die by water, who would die of disease." People who had wronged someone during the year would seek them out for forgiveness, even if on the following day "they would be cutting each other's throats again." But on this Yom Kippur, the cutting of throats was no longer a metaphor, and death was nearer to everyone.

Normally it was a day of joy. Of family, food and prayer. The Willners observed this Yom Kippur in the quiet confines of their home with the windows closed and curtains pulled. A few friends had joined them and risked being shot if caught outdoors after sundown. The only food was potatoes and a small chunk of beef that had been hidden from the Germans. At any moment the front door could be broken down and soldiers on top of them. To hold such a celebration with a group of people would be looked at as resistance to the rule of law, the twisted rule of Nazi law where justice had no place. To even hint of resistance in any form meant certain death. Still, it was held, with one person always peering out the window as a lookout. Afterwards, the friends and family silently snuck home and the Willners retired to bed in a chilly house with no wood to burn for heat. They were also going to bed with hunger. A gnawing emptiness that was never satisfied and never squelched. The body's demands to go on, even if it has no fuel to burn. The life force is not so easily extinguished.

That night Kalman dreamt of his grandmother and grandfather. She was holding a bucket full of red apples and he was standing behind her with a handful of candy. As Kalman started to walk toward them, the apples turned into blood and the candy into bullets and then they disappeared. Kalman woke up in a cold sweat and began to cry softly into his pillow. He stayed awake until sunrise when he left the house to work. His father was too ill and Kalman volunteered to work for the family. If for some reason he did not show up for work with his papers, the whole family risked death.

the hole

As the days and weeks passed, Kalman and Chiel worked the farms which had been taken over by the Germans. Even though they risked their own lives they were still able to snatch a few potatoes for the family. Sometimes a radish or turnip. Their father's Polish friends also would sneak them a few eggs or fresh milk when they could, but it was becoming more difficult and dangerous and the food slowly stopped coming in.

On a cold, October morning with the smell of harvest in the air, news came that there had been a massacre in a small village 20 kilometers north of Dombrowa. The details were sketchy and many people initially put it off as hysteria until the only surviving witness appeared within the confines of their village. A bedraggled man who appeared to be in his 40's or 50's, with a day old beard of black stubble and equally black circles under his wild eyes, came into town. He was half-crazed and seemed to be possessed by an evil spirit. He half walked and half ran through the village telling people of what he saw. "A German soldier had disappeared and they rounded up everyone in the village and asked where the soldier was and no one knew and they asked and asked and no one knew, no one knew! How could they know?! The soldier was gone and no one knew where he was and they couldn't find him and the officer said he had disappeared and that something had happened to him and that we knew, that we knew and that we had taken him and we knew but would not tell." He spoke without breathing, as if his last breath had already been used and he was now walking and talking breathless. "They made everyone dig a hole – a giant hole - and again the officer asked where the soldier was but we could not tell because we did not know." The man then began to weep. "They made us dig a hole and he said if we did not tell him what he wanted to know the hole would become our grave. Children and their parents were crying...begging...but he would not listen. The officer said this will be a lesson to you all and the soldiers began pushing people into the hole...whole families into the hole; men, women, children....then....oh my god....they buried them! They buried 20 people alive! You could hear their screams until it was muffled by the dirt and then there was nothing but silence."

"And you," someone had asked. "Why were you not buried?"

"I am a barber," the man told them, staring ahead with his wild eyes. "I cut the officer's hair and for that he spared me. He told me I must go to all the villages and tell the people what will happen to them if a soldier is killed. They told me to warn you that if one soldier is killed a hundred of you will be killed, and after that a thousand....and after that....." and the man collapsed onto the street.

A few days later they found the soldier. He had been with a Polish girl. But the warning remained.

How could anyone have so much hatred? Kalman asked himself over and over and over. *Did they not see what loving, giving human beings these people are that are being butchered like pigs? That they were mothers and brothers and sisters and wives and sons and daughters? Do they not care?* But there were no answers. No "whys". It simply was. The life of his family and friends meant no more than moldy bread to the Gestapo, and the only thing to do was survive.

protect ourselves

Each ensuing week brought more terror to the village of Dombrowa. The main Gestapo headquarters was in Tarnow, but a small garrison remained in Dombrowa. Once or twice a week word would come that a company was coming from headquarters. The townspeople were alerted by the "live telephone". All communications in and out of Dombrowa had been cut, but any news gathered by various Jewish groups in the outlying towns would be passed along mainly by small boys who would run to a specified area and pass off the information to another boy who would then take it to yet another spot until it had reached its destination.

Any news that the Germans were coming usually meant one of two things; either they would be demanding more money or more men to work or both. But more and more frequently it meant more shootings. The troops would arrive inconspicuously, round up a group of people and shoot them with no apparent reason. The organization of the Nazi killing machine was staggering. Constant uncertainty and gnawing anxiety filtered through the town and never, ever went away. Anxiety and fear became Dombrowa's and the Willner's constant companion.

When Kalman went to work each morning he could only hope that when he returned home his family would still be there, for there were now one hundred to one hundred fifty people taken from town each week, never to be seen again. The stakes were getting higher and Mr. Willner along with other families devised plans to escape the SS.

It was grandma Willner who first pointed it out to her son.

"Herschl, do you really think they are taking these people to work? And why do not they come back? Are they still working? In the first war the armies were set upon destroying each other, but now, now....these animals are set upon destroying us. Are we to sit and wait for them to gather us up like your cattle to take us to the slaughter?"

Mr. Willner knew she was right and that evening he took Kalman and Chiel aside.

"We must protect ourselves any way we can. Your mother

and I have decided that when the Gestapo is approaching, you boys will take Moshe and run to the woods. You know those woods better than the birds that live in them. There you will be safe. We will take Sarah and go to the other side of town beyond the cemetery. When all is clear and the action is over we will meet back here. Do you understand?"

"Yes father," they answered quietly.

"And if the Germans are too close to run we will hide in the basement, there we will have a chance of not being found."

He looked at the boys and his face seemed to have aged 30 years from worry and concern. If he could have, he would have taken the family and put them under his own skin, close to his heart, where he could watch over them and protect them, but he knew he could not, and that ate away at him without mercy.

"Come," he told the boys. "Come here."

Kalman and Chiel got up and stepped over to where their father was sitting. Without speaking, Mr. Willner reached up and gently wrapped his arms around the boys, pulling them closely to his side. He held them tightly and wished this moment never to end, to be close to his boys, to have his family tucked away safely under his roof.

"I love you very much," he told them. "Never forget that."

After their father had gone to bed, the two boys sat around the wood stove which was cold and still. Chiel looked at his older brother and asked, "What will happen to us Kalman?"

"I don't know Chiel," Kalman replied. "I don't know, but we must listen to papa. We must watch over each other. Stay close. That is what grandfather would have wanted. He said we would be OK. He would not lie."

blood red moon

In the early morning twilight, Venus kissed the lip of the Cheshire moon, a silver grin beneath a shadowy globe. For millennia the moon had born witness to man's folly and miracle, from the rise of civilization in Mesopotamia to the fall of the Egyptians, Romans, and the hidden kingdoms of the Anasazi, Aztecs and Mayans. It hung in the sky and gave light unto Jesus, Mohammed, Confucius and the Buddha. Its light reflected off the pristine marble of Michelangelo's David and Van Gogh's Sunflowers. It had seen the coming of the Huns and Mongols, constant wars and an industrial revolution, but never had it witnessed carnage the likes of this Century, and as this 20th Century approached its forth decade, the moon turned blood red.

Grandmother Willner awoke to the tell-tale sounds of jeeps and half-tracks rumbling in the distance and her heart began to race. Then came a knock at the door. Kalman got up to answer it, but before he reached the door, his father rushed out of the bedroom. "Stay away from the door!" he shouted with a forceful whisper.

Kalman stepped back and Mr. Willner slowly approached the door. Mrs. Willner stood by the bedroom holding onto Sarah while Chiel and Moshe sat on the bed with grandmother.

Again a knock came upon the door, this time louder and faster. Mr. Willner turned the knob and the door flung open from the outside. Standing on the rickety wooden porch were the Goldman sisters and coming up behind them were Mr. Goldman and his wife. The girls looked as though they had just fallen out of bed, their nightgowns still on, hair ruffled, and very, very frightened.

"The SS are coming," the oldest one said. "Big Gestapo…" she continued, but before she could finish her sentence, Mr. Goldman had joined them on the porch.

"She's right Herschl. They're already here – main Gestapo – it's not good – not good," he said nervously.

"Come in girls," Mr. Willner said as he motioned the Goldmans into the house. "Everyone come in – hurry! Do the others know?"

"I think so," Mr. Goldman replied. "I think so."

Meanwhile grandma Willner had moved the dining table and rug away from a trap door that led to the cellar. Within a few minutes there were twenty to thirty people in the house including friends, family and neighbors. Everyone seemed frantic, knocking into furniture, bumping into each other, some silent and others walking around with a frenetic pace.

"What's going on mama?" Moshe asked, old enough to understand fear, but too young to comprehend the danger.

"I'm scared," "Sarah added as she began to cry softly.

"Everybody!" Mr. Willner shouted loudly. "You must get into the cellar. There is no time to waste.

Mrs. Willner took the young ones and began leading them to the trap door. Moshe was afraid of closed places and did not want to go, but grandmother pleaded with him gently. "Come Moshe, it will be OK. Rabbits live in holes and they are not afraid. You will be safe down there, I won't let anything happen to you, I promise. Listen to your grandma now."

With grandma's persuasion, Moshe was led downstairs by Kalman and Chiel. The last two remaining people upstairs were

Mr. Willner and grandmother.

"Now you must go down mother."

"And you, what will you do?"

"I will be the bait. They will see me and I can distract them. We have already discussed this."

"And what do you think they'll do once they find you? A man sitting alone in his house? You are as good as dead if you stay up here."

"It has to be this way."

"No it doesn't Herschl. I won't allow it. I will stay up here. I am no threat to them."

"I won't allow it. No."

"You can't stop me. If you stay I will stay with you and we will both be killed. Is that what you want?"

Sporadic gunfire could be heard in town along with yelling and screaming.

"They're getting closer," Zisla told her son. "You must go down now while there's still time."

"Come, Herschl," he heard from downstairs. "She's right, hurry or we'll all be dead."

"Daddy," a voice cried out. "I don't want to be alone down here. Daddy come down, please." It was Sarah.

Mr. Willner looked at his mother.

"Listen to her Herschl. Now go."

He continued to look at his mother, at this woman who had carried him in her womb, raised and fed and loved him and he was torn apart. Again Sarah called out, "Daddy!"

"Go my son; go before it's too late."

He grabbed his mother and hugged her tightly and didn't

want to let her go, he wanted to hold her forever, but she gently pushed him away. "Go now," she told him once more.

Finally he pulled away from her and started to descend the narrow steps. He looked up once more at his mother. She smiled faintly at him with great sorrow in her eyes as her son disappeared beneath the floor. The cellar was damp and musty. The trap door closed. A small candle flickered in the corner, casting eerie shadows onto the subterranean captives like a group of hidden specters.

Before long, they heard footsteps clomping on the wooden floor, heavy, rushed steps, steps made by boots. The young children were hushed by their mothers who placed their hands over their mouths. Upstairs grandmother sat on a wooden chair next to the stove while a Gestapo officer stood in front of her.

"Where are the stinking Jews?" he shouted as spittle formed on the corner of his mouth. He was a piggish looking man with a round face and heavy jowls. His lips were nearly purple and this made him appear somewhat hypoxic, as if the oxygen in his brain had been cut off for a bit too long. Again he shouted vehemently; "Where are the stinking Jews?"

"*Sie arbeiten,*" she said in perfect German but with a Yiddish accent. "They are working."

"You lie you old sow!"

From the cellar they could hear crashing sounds as the soldiers began turning the house upside down. They threw Sarah's old stroller into a cupboard, smashing old plates and cups, the jagged pieces falling onto a homemade doll the boys had made for their little sister. Then they heard the kitchen table being turned over as it crashed into the floor. The only thing separating them and the SS was a flimsy rug and a trap door. If they were found hiding they would surely all be killed on the spot.

Grandmother Willner didn't move a muscle as they continued to ransack the house, nor did she blink an eye as they turned the table over. After the men had searched all through the house, the piggish officer went into a rage and began screaming at grandmother. From the cellar they could hear feet kicking over the floor as grandmother was being dragged out of the house. The front door opened and slammed shut. Then they could hear shouting in the street but could not make out what was being said.

Then a gunshot rang out, a horrible, compressive noise; a noise that set the nerves on fire. Then another...and another....and in the end, a total of five shots cut through the air. Five shots from a .38 caliber Luger to kill one old woman. Mr. Willner went wild and had to be held down by ten men. He wanted to rush out onto the street and kill the soldiers – to kill them all with his bare hands, but the others understood that to do so would mean all of their demise. "No, no, no!" he cried out, finally collapsing onto the floor.

"There was nothing you could do," his wife tried to console him, but Kalman knew as he watched the nightmarish scene unfold that nothing could ever console his father, and he also knew that he had just lost his last remaining grandparent. He stood in silence and his body felt numb. He wished it would all go away. He felt utter, complete powerlessness and was ashamed for his own self-pity and helplessness while so much suffering was going on around him. He felt as though he was standing in a tomb of the doomed.

Several hours passed before the people arose from the cellar, making sure that all was clear, they ascended the steps, walked through the house which was now torn apart, and peered out the windows. Seeing no one in the streets, Mr. Willner ran out onto the narrow dirt road in front of the house, and there where his mother had stood was nothing but a puddle of blood which had leached through the dirt and begun to dry. Her body was surely lying in a trench together with others who had met the same fate, and the thought of this was too much to bear.

"God is punishing us....God is punishing us...." Mr. Willner mumbled over and over and over. Still, Kalman could not believe that God would do such a thing. He remembered what his grandfather had told him after the shootings in the Market Square, but what did it matter? What did it matter if this was God's doing or the Devil's? Or just man's? Or the evil *in* man? The outcome was the same. To suffer.

Kalman found Sarah's doll beneath shards of glass, broken plates and cups. He bent over to pick it up and lying next to it was a red handkerchief. It had been placed in an old canister by his mother and fell out onto the floor when the canister broke. The kerchief had belonged to grandfather. He used to wipe his nose after taking a pinch of snuff and then he would use it to bless the children. Kalman placed it into his pocket and grabbed the doll. Sarah was sitting on the bed in the corner of the room where grandma Willner once slept. Sarah's shoulders were stooped forward and her head hung low. She looked at the ground and said nothing. Kalman walked over and sat next to her on the bed. He handed her the doll but she looked at it as if she had never seen it before. Then a tiny spark lit in her expressionless eyes as she looked up at Kalman and took the doll from his hand and held it close to her chest. She rocked it back and forth and a tiny smile came across her lips.

The gathered friends and family pulled Mr. Willner off the street and helped him back inside the house. He sat on a flimsy wooden chair next to the wood stove while the others cleaned the house and put everything back in order the best they could. All the silver and other valuables had been taken, but still, if only they could put the house back together, then it would be as it once was, and the memory would fade, but for Mr. Willner, it would never fade. Never. The only thing of true value was family, friends, and God. And day by day each was disappearing, one by one.

CHAPTER 5

the beating snow

Fall rapidly turned to winter and a light snow covered the village. The wind blew ice crystals across the ground in little swirls that bit the skin as it the face. Kalman worked each day for the Germans, as did Chiel. Rations were becoming short, and hunger began following the family with its constant, nagging claws. One arose with emptiness in the stomach and went to bed with the same. Sarah and Moshe became dangerously thin and constantly complained of "tummy aches." Mr. Willner's ulcers had worsened to the point that on many days he could barely stand up. Kalman often experienced nausea and headaches, and fatigue began to set in. Often while working he felt as though he were wading through quicksand with cement boots, his head pounding and his stomach gurgling.

On a cold, gray day toward the end of 1939, word came from the live telephone that a large group of SS was on their way to Dombrowa. Mr. and Mrs. Willner took the two younger children and ran out past the cemetery while Kalman and Chiel took to the woods. Just as the two boys entered the border of the forest where they would be hidden by the trees, a small group of soldiers spotted them.

"Halt!" the Germans shouted. "Stop right there!"

The boys started to run.

The SS blew a warning whistle to alert the others and continued yelling for them to stop. Then they started shooting into the woods. Kalman felt a bullet whiz past his ear. Trees were exploding all around them as hot lead tore into the soft wood. Chiel was jumping over logs and high stepping snow bluffs with his knees kicking up like pistons. Kalman was wearing wooden shoes and the snow kept getting stuck to them, turning his feet into large clumps of snow and ice. To make matters worse, the snow was beginning to soften under the afternoon sun, causing the snowy shoes to stick to the snow-covered ground like glue. Each time he tried to pick up his leg another big clump of snow and branches came with it. The soldiers were getting closer, but Kalman could not run any faster no matter how hard he tried. Sweat was pouring off his forehead and soaked through his shirt. He could hear the Germans on the other side of the hill right below him. Chiel was yelling at him to run faster as the snowy shoes got caught in a large pile of slushy snow and Kalman fell flat on his face.

"Get up Kalman! Hurry! Get up!" Chiel yelled.

Kalman tried to push himself up, but his arms kept sinking beneath the snow. Finally he managed to get to his feet by hoisting himself up by a branch. Just as he started to heave himself through the snow, the Germans rounded the hill.

"There he is!" They shouted. "Get him!"

Kalman felt like he was in a dream where he was being chased but his legs would not move. He struggled to move faster, but was no match for the soldiers. He could feel them getting closer, though he refused to look back. He wished he could jump out of his body so it wouldn't slow him down any longer, but it was already too late. He felt a powerful thud across his back which knocked the wind out of him and forced him to the ground. Then a boot stomped on the middle of his back, thrusting his body and face into the snow, which made it even harder to breathe. The soldiers were yelling and screaming, but Kalman in his fear and excitement and with snow plugging his ears, could not make out what they were saying. Chiel could do nothing but watch, and when he saw his brother being stomped into the snow he took off running again and disappeared behind the tree's and hills. The only thing louder than the yelling Germans was a squirrel that was sitting high atop a tree above the soldiers. It screeched loudly from all the commotion and seemed almost to be screaming at the soldiers. One of the men took aim at the furry animal and shot at it with his rifle. The bullet missed and the squirrel ran around to the other side of the tree, screeching all the way.

"Nice shot idiot!" one of the soldiers told the marksman.

"Yes, but I won't miss this rodent," he yelled back as he kicked Kalman in the stomach, knocking the air out of him once more. "Him I will hit dead on."

The others then grabbed Kalman by the arms and roughly pulled him out of the snow. Kalman felt as though his shoulders were going to dislocate as they drug him out. Snow covered his face and melted into his eyes, which made his vision blurry. All he could see was an outline of his captors. He was gasping for breath and his wooden shoes had been yanked off his feet when they drug him out and his toes stung like fire from the cold.

"You think you can run from us you little swine!"

Then came the fists. Hard, balled up fists pounding into his face. He could here the crack of white knuckles across his cheek bones, his jaw, his ears and body. The pounding vibrated through his head and nearly deafened him. Then an elbow or fist or foot caught his nose and Kalman was sure it had been completely smashed – flattened against his face. He could feel the blood pour out of his nose and drain onto his shirt. He was becoming disoriented. A skinny, fourteen year old boy in the middle of the forest being severely beaten by a group of crazed adults. The civilized world.

"Why are they doing this? Why? Why? What have I done?" Kalman asked himself in the back of his mind. He asked this not with words, but with his spirit, his gut, his essence as a human being. *Why? What have I done?*

After being viciously pummeled, Kalman was drug into an opening in the forest where fifteen to twenty other escapees had been gathered. They were all sitting in the snow on the ground with armed soldiers standing over them. Kalman was pushed down between two captives, and the group was tied and bound together with rope. They were then forced to lie on the ground while the soldiers circled them and discussed with great glee and pleasure what they were to do with the prisoners.

"We should shoot them now," one of the men would say.

"And waste bullets?" another would reply.

Kalman hurt all over and felt his face begin to swell. If not for the snow and the cold air his eyes surely would have swelled shut. For what seemed like hours, the SS tormented the group when finally one of the officers cocked his rifle. The bolt locked into the chamber with a hard, deep clang and he began circling the group. He walked up to a young woman and put the rifle to her head; the cold metal of the barrel touching her temple.

"Hmm," the officer said with a sadistic air. "What would this bullet do to that pretty little head?"

The woman was shaking on the ground and began to cry.

"Oh, I see," the officer continued. "Now you cry. You should have thought of that before you ran."

His finger curled around the trigger. Kalman could see it in the corner of his eye. The officer's finger tightened and the trigger pulled.

Clack!

The chamber was empty. The young woman burst out in tears and sobbed uncontrollably.

The soldiers were laughing as the officer continued to walk around the captives.

"I know there are bullets in here. Question is…where?"

For over an hour he randomly walked from person to person and pointed the rifle at their heads.

"Maybe this is the one," he said as he repeatedly pulled the trigger. Each time the bolt clacked an empty chamber. The hour stretched into most of the day and felt like an eternity as the people were subjected to a sinister game of life and death.

How will it feel to die? Will it hurt? My family? Will I never see them again?

These thoughts, together with feelings of excruciating anxiety and sadness grew with each passing second until finally the officer screamed; "Get up! Get up now before I shoot you all!"

The terrified, brutalized captives were then gathered together and carted away on a horse driven wagon that had been confiscated from a Polish farmer. The rickety wagon made its way down a narrow road which led to town. Kalman sat near the back of the wagon. He had decided that if they were going to the cemetery to be shot he would jump out of the wagon and run. Better to be shot while running than gunned down in a grave yard. But the wagon passed the cemetery and headed straight into town where the group was incarcerated in a small jail. The jail cell was roughly 10 by 15 feet in size and the group was herded into it like cattle. There were two old mattresses and a cement floor. With all the people packed in, there was barely enough room to sit. One toilet sat in the middle of the room and this was especially humiliating to the women who had to relieve themselves. Kalman sat quietly in a corner. Walls of protection slowly rose within him. His body was in the cell but everything else withdrew inside, inside where it's safe.

Don't let them touch you – inside – where it's safe. Protected.

Don't let them touch you inside – where I dwell. What they see is not me – can not be. Will not be!
Remain invisible.

They sat in the cage throughout the night. The building was cold but the heat emanating from the bodies and damp clothes made the cell feel sticky. By morning a sickly sweet smell filled the building from all the closely packed bodies. No one knew whether they would live or die. No food was given. No water. People were growing panicky from the close confinement and thirst and hunger. Kalman was in so much pain from the beating that he could barely stand.

A few hours after sunrise three soldiers came to the cell, opened the door and told them all to get out.

"Get out of here! Go home!"

The disbelieving prisoners were dazed and thought it must be a trick. Two men helped Kalman to his feet. "Come now boy, it's time to go."

They all left the building and wondered if they would all be shot on the street, but instead, their families were waiting for them. The council and villagers had arranged their release with a ransom. They were saved. This time.

Kalman spent several days in bed. His face and body turned from black and blue to purple and yellow. "You look like a rainbow," his mother teased him, trying to raise his spirits. His muscles and joints felt like rusty bolts when he moved, but slowly he got back onto his feet and his young body healed. Yet he would never forget the beating.

bricks at pustkow

Kalman's bruises faded and the winter snows melted. The spring runoff brought forth new life to the woods. Wild flowers bloomed, berry bushes sprouted, new grass began to coat the damp earth. It also exposed corpses buried beneath the snow, frozen still in the moment of their death with twisted limbs and hollow, anguished faces. Kalman was now fifteen and Chiel thirteen. They had spent the good part of the winter working on various farms and as laborers for the Nazis. In the depth of the cold, winter months, the SS activities slowed down. The Jewish population was still required to work, but interaction with the Germans was minimal.

In May of 1940, a large number of young boys, including the two Willner brothers, were rounded up and brought to the Gymnasium, the Polish high school of town. They stood in formation while two SS officers walked through the room pointing to various boys, after which two soldiers would immediately grab them and pull them over to the other side of the room. Both Kalman and Chiel were picked – for what they did not know.

After the selection had been made, the officer yelled, "All of you. You will come with us." And that was it. Without forewarning or explanation, the gathered group of roughly fifty young boys and teenagers were filed onto a large truck and taken away. They were not allowed to speak to their families. No one in the village knew where they were going or that they were even taken until hours later.

For several hours they were driven over rough roads, their young, thin bodies and bony butts bouncing off the hard metal bed of the truck. The smell of exhaust was thick and heavy. Several boys succumbed to severe headaches and began to vomit while clutching their heads with their hands. Even in the comfort of your own home, in the dark and quiet of your own bed, a blinding headache can be debilitating. Perhaps your mother would place a cold compress on your forehead and gently massage your temples, but in the back of a truck with nothing but hard, cold metal to lean on, with the noise of the engine pounding your head and exhaust filling your lungs; all the while being taken to an unknown spot by men who would more likely kick your head than massage it; such a headache was unbearable - unbearable because of the great vulnerability it imparted. Void of compassion and caring, such a headache can kill.

Vulnerability and sadness hovered over all the boys and was only surpassed by great trepidation and anxiety. The boys would try to comfort each other but they were all afraid. Kalman missed his family and worried about his mother and father.

"If only I could have said goodbye," he thought to himself. "Just to tell them goodbye, just to see them one more time. If only..." But at least he had his brother by his side.

Finally they arrived in Pustkow, a small village in SE Poland. Several villages in the area had been evacuated and destroyed to make way for a large SS training camp that was being built. As soon as the truck stopped, the soldiers started yelling, hurrying the boys out of the truck. Kalman leg's felt stiff from sitting for hours and his knees nearly buckled when he jumped off the truck. The boys were forced to stand in formation once again, five in a row, and Kalman stood in the middle. They were counted and given succinct instructions.

"You were brought here to work. If you work, you will live. If you do not, you will die. Any attempt to escape is futile. If you are caught trying to escape, you will be hanged. Do you understand?"

The boys stood silently.

"Good," the commandant continued. "We understand each other perfectly then."

Pustkow was in a heavily wooded area and not easily seen from the air. The grounds were made up of several rectangular brick buildings, including one very large structure that appeared to be a half-finished munitions house, along with a small open area of grass and mud. The boys were taken to one of the buildings and fed a small cup of watery soup with a slice of turnip floating in it. After the meal, the boys were led to their rooms. Each room housed ten boys. There was nothing but bare brick walls, a cement floor with a thin layer of straw and bare windowpanes. The open window let the cold night air pass through, but Kalman and Chiel welcomed the fresh air after being nearly asphyxiated by the truck's exhaust.

It was already dusk and everyone was told to stay in their rooms until told otherwise.

"How long will they keep us here?"

"What will they do with us?"

These were the questions echoing through every brick room.

Questions without answers.

Kalman and Chiel slept fitfully if at all. They were like cats sleeping with one eye open. Always on guard. Always anticipating the unexpected. And though their bodies were tired and their minds fatigued, they were unable to rest as an anxious weariness set in.

In the pre-dawn hour the building was awakened by the shriek of loud whistles and harsh commands spat out in guttural German. The guards went into each room, yelling and kicking at the boys' feet, grabbing them by the hair or arms and yanking them to their feet.

"Get up you lazy swine!" the guards yelled. "Do you think this is a vacation? Do I look like your mother?" they laughed. "I am much prettier than your mother!"

After the guards left, Chiel said, "If my mother were as ugly as he I would cut my own head off." All the boys laughed.

Everyone was then shuffled outside and forced to stand in formation to be counted. The group was methodically split off into smaller groups and then led away by guards. The guard in charge of Kalman and Chiel's group stopped the two brothers and asked them how old they were. They both had baby faces without even a hint of stubble on their chins.

"I am fifteen," Kalman answered. "And he is thirteen."

The guard, no older than nineteen himself, looked at them for a moment and slowly shook his head.

"Come now," he said. "We have work to do."

Kalman gazed around the camp. It was still in the process of being built and loosely guarded. There were no watchtowers, no barbed-wire fence; only a small patch of open ground surrounded by a deep forest. From sun-up to sundown Kalman and his brother carried bricks from one end of the camp to the other. Their hands quickly blistered and stung from handling the rough bricks. Kalman could feel the muscles between his shoulders blades begin to spasm. His low back and biceps burned from fatigue under the constant, heavy weight. At noon they would be fed a small piece of sour bread, perhaps a spot of cabbage soup, and then sent back to work. On occasion they would be given a piece of *blutwürst*, a sausage made primarily of fat and blood stuffed into a tube of intestine, but their meager food never provided enough calories even for a sedentary lifestyle, let alone for the fuel burnt by their heavy labor. Soon their bodies felt heavy and burdened.

This meant nothing to the SS, however, the boys could be beaten because they carried fifteen bricks instead of twenty, or perhaps for no reason at all. Kalman watched two or three boys literally beaten to death. On one rainy day near nightfall, one of the boys who had been prone to headaches was now getting thin and gaunt and began to wear down towards the end of the day. His legs were tiring under the weight of the bricks and he kept getting stuck in the mud. Each time he fell, a sadistic guard would come up to him with a stick and start beating him on the back until he got up. At one point the boy fell in a large mud puddle and dropped all of the bricks in the process. Before he even had a chance to get up the guard was on top of him like a rabid beast, beating him with a stick and shoving his face in the mud with his boots. Kalman watched as the boy blew his last bubbles of breath in the frothy, muddy water. The boy's body became limp and the guard simply walked away. The boy had slept with the brothers the previous night. He was a gifted young artist. He made figures out of straw and mud, that is all he wanted to do, and as he created each new piece with his blistered fingers, he seemed to be far away from the camp and the guards, but art had no place here, and now neither did he, except in the open grave of an old ditch.

Kalman was careful not to let the guard notice him, for his rage would surely be turned on him. All he could do was keep working.

"Just work and don't slow down," he kept telling himself.

"Just keep working and they won't notice."

On their tenth day at Pustkow, Chiel was taken aside by one of the officers who had taken a liking to him. He was given a job taking care of the officer's horses, allowed to sleep in the stables, which was a step above the hard cement floor of the barracks, and he was given better food to eat. He didn't want to leave his brother, but Kalman convinced him to go.

"Just do what they ask," Kalman told Chiel. "Take care of yourself and don't worry about me. We'll meet up soon."

Reluctantly, Chiel agreed. He really had no choice in the matter, but even the illusion of choice can make an impossible situation somewhat more palatable.

Each day the guards became more violent. Kalman was so hungry that he often ate grass just to fend off stomach pains. There was no bathhouse, no outhouse, and every day a crazed guard killed another boy. He missed his family greatly and thought of them constantly.

Finally, after three weeks at the work camp, Kalman had had enough. He lay awake the night before thinking of home. He remembered the Sabbaths spent with his family before the madness. Days without worry. Roast chicken and sweet breads and pickled herring - and he knew he would leave that very night. He must return home!

After a breakfast of burnt chicory and water, the boys went back out into the fields. For the last several days they had been cutting down trees, digging out the roots with makeshift tools and hauling the trunks away to be burnt. Today Kalman was to be back on brick detail. The brick pile was at the periphery of camp near the trees. At dusk as they were finishing up, Kalman walked across the flats and headed to the bricks with a wheelbarrow. Once he got there, he slipped out behind the pile and walked steadily into the woods. His heart was racing and he could feel eyes on him but he never looked back. Once hidden behind the trees he started running. He ran as fast as he could through the moist foliage and never looked back. He walked and ran through the woods all through the night, finally stopping at a bend in a creek where he leaned up against a large boulder to rest.

His pants were shredded from the thorny bushes and branches and his thin leather shoes were falling off his feet. Occasionally he would catch a drift of his own body odor and it smelled sour and sweet - a mixture of sweat, mud, mortar and fear. Fear has its own smell. He could smell it on his hands and it nearly made him sick. Driven forward by the sheer anticipation of seeing his family again, and fearful that they would not be there when he returned, Kalman walked until he came upon an old, brick farmhouse. It belonged to a Jewish family which had lived there for generations. He approached the house cautiously and looked inside. A woman saw him peering in the window. She winced with fright. Looking again, she saw that Kalman was only a boy, and motioned him to come inside.

"What are you doing out here in the middle of the night," the woman asked.

"I was in Pustkow and ran away," Kalman answered.

The husband then walked into the room and looked at Kalman.

"He escaped the camp," the woman told her husband.

"I see," the husband replied. "How long have you been running?"

"Most of the night," Kalman answered quietly.

"Well, I'm afraid, my son, that you have gotten turned around. Pustkow is less the one kilometer from here. You have been going in circles."

Kalman couldn't believe it. If he would have continued on his path he would have walked right back into his captor's hands. Before he could speak, the wife broke in, "Come, you look exhausted. Sit and I will get you something to eat." She fed him a bowl of warm borscht and her husband set him up in the barn with a wool blanket and feather pillow.

"In the morning you will have to leave," the husband told him. "If they catch you here we will all be killed. I have two young children. I will draw you a map so you won't get lost again"

"Thank you," Kalman told him before promptly falling asleep.

At dawn Kalman set out again. He followed the map around a river and down quiet roads so as not to draw attention. He slept in an open wheat field the second evening and ate raw wheat to fend off his hunger. Finally after two days of walking he reached Dombrowa.

Rather than going straight to his house, he first went to an uncle's place on the edge of town. He was afraid the SS would be looking for him and did not want to jeopardize his family's safety. His uncle greeted him with great surprise. "Kalman! You're alive!" his uncle kept shouting gleefully. "Where have you been? What did they do with you? And your brother? Where is he?"

Kalman told him of the camp at Pustkow and that Chiel was living in a stable and taking care of an officer's horses. What Kalman wanted to know, but was almost afraid to ask, was if his family was still in the village.

"Mama? And papa? Are they OK? And Sarah and Moshe?" He asked cautiously. He was afraid of the answer. What would he do if they were gone? He couldn't bear to think about it.

His uncle grabbed Kalman firmly by the shoulders, looked him straight in the eyes, and said with a big smile on his face; "They're OK Kalman. They're all safe. You must wait until evening and we will go see them."

where god dwells

That evening, Kalman and his uncle ventured over to the house. Kalman looked around the town, saddened by its emptiness. Many people had already been taken away, and the spirit of the village seemed to be vanishing. As he approached the house, however, his melancholy was replaced by great anticipation. He could see the kerosene lantern glowing through the kitchen window and knew now his family truly was home – and alive!

They knocked at the door quietly so as not to frighten the family. When his father opened the door and saw Kalman he began to cry. Without speaking he grabbed his son and held him tightly. His mother came in from the kitchen and saw the three standing at the doorway. "Kalman my son!" she cried out. "Kalman – oh my Kalman!"

His parents seemed to have aged ten years since he left. Heavy lines and dark shadows circled their eyes, but the light that shone out of them on this night seemed to transcend the dark circles somehow, just as the light of an oncoming train breaks through the darkness of a tunnel.

Kalman ran in and hugged his mother, the warmth of her love enveloping him in a warm shroud of comfort. Moshe then came up to hug his big brother, followed by Sarah. Within her hands, she held the old doll Kalman had made for her. The same doll he later saved from the shards of glass the day grandmother Willner was killed. Sarah handed the doll to Kalman. He grabbed the doll, then picked Sarah up and gave her a big kiss on the cheek.

For one evening, the Nazi occupation vanished from the Willner household.

The Spirit of God lived that day through the Willner's joy and in their love of one another.

CHAPTER 6

naked humanness

Nostalgia is a reflection of bygone days. Moments of a life once lived. Glimpses of past loves and losses, friends and foe, of what was and may have been.

Nostalgia is belated thanks for one's life; gratitude in retrospect.

One has only to lose his life to wish he had it back again.

Kalman caught a glimpse of that life upon his return to Dombrowa from the camp at Pustkow. For a fifteen year old or a one hundred fifteen year old who has suffered loss and separation, nostalgia is a strange bedfellow - an old friend who brings a smile with a tear and joy with sadness.

The corner where grandmother Willner's bed had stood was empty now. The bakery where grandma Kohane had bent over kneading dough until the crook in her back became permanent, was now run by a fat German-Pole whose cigarette ashes and sweat dripped into the flat, tasteless breads he made. There was no school and the Synagogue had been taken over by the Gestapo. Houses of friends stood empty. Many people developed a far away look in their eyes, an empty stare, vacant and numb. At times an emptiness as cold and void as the vacuum of space would pass through Kalman. A vacuum from which their seemed to be no escape.

Kalman could not stay with his parents for fear the SS would search for him, so he slept at his uncle Shilek's house and saw his family only briefly during the day. The Jewish Council put him back to work on the farms. The days turned into weeks and the weeks into months. Just as a young bird nesting beneath a massive granite boulder perched precariously upon a narrow ledge could be crushed without warning, so it was in Dombrowa, as life stretched hour to hour, moment to moment, ready to collapse without warning and come crashing down upon the villagers.

Spring passed into the blistering days of summer. The work was long and heavy, yet being alone in the fields under an open sky gave Kalman a sense, however brief, of freedom. Keeping the body busy prevented the mind from spinning rapidly out of control.

In the autumn of 1940, as the days grew shorter and the evenings cooler, Kalman was approaching the springtime of his adolescence. A rain of hormones flowed through his veins. His thoughts turned often towards a young girl - the shimmer of her walnut hair under the sun - the softness of her face and the roundness of her bottom beneath a light cotton dress. Even under the power of great evil, desire is not so easily extinguished. They exchanged glances while passing on the street. In time these glances became shy smiles. They were careful not to let the Germans witness any of it, for to draw attention to themselves meant humiliation at best, and beating or death at worst.

The girl was a friend of the Goldman sisters, and they persuaded Kalman to talk to her. "Come on Kalman, she likes you," they prompted.

So finally one day as the two were passing in the street, Kalman stopped her and said hello. His voice was a little shaky and she tended to giggle a lot, but they both fumbled through their initial jitters and became good friends. When it was safe, they would meet and talk about what they would do when the war was over. Even if they didn't believe it ever would or could be over, they were able to convince themselves of it while together, and that in itself was a great gift.

One Sunday afternoon, Kalman convinced her to venture out into the woods. She declined at first, but Kalman was persistent. He first brought her to the tree where he and Sarah had carved their initials. Then they looked for wild berries, picked them fresh off the shrubs until their fingers were stained purple, and then sat beneath a large oak tree. They held hands. Then the girl reached over and kissed Kalman on the cheek, making him all warm and tingly inside. For a brief moment they were alone together, with nothing else in the world but them and the tree and the berries and the kiss - and it was magical!

Out of the quiet, they heard a rustling in the leaves, and the moment was broken. Kalman leaped up quickly, "Ssshhh!" He told his companion. "Stay there and don't get up." He peered around the tree and scanned the woods but saw nothing. Then they heard the rustling again. It seemed to be coming from a pocket of willows directly in front of them.

"Kalman, I'm scared."

"Just stay here. If we stay behind the tree they won't see us. I think they're coming from the willows."

Again they heard the rustle of leaves and the whisper of moving grass, but this time it was closer. Kalman peeked around the tree, and just as he did, the willows and tall grass began to shake.

"Someone's coming," he whispered.

He sat transfixed onto the patch of brush when out of the thicket walked a red fox and her three cubs, oblivious to the two frightened kids hiding behind the tree. Kalman plopped down on his butt and sighed with a smile.

"What is it?" The girl asked. "Who is it? What's going on?" she insisted.

"It's a fox…the big bad wolf," Kalman laughed.

He turned to look at the girl and saw that she was trembling. Then he noticed a spot of blood on her dress. The fear of the moment had started her period. Kalman pretended not to notice. Her thin legs were stretched out from underneath her dress, the sharp bones of her shins exposed beneath a thin layer of muscle and skin. She could feel her blood drip into the ground. Flesh and bone, soil and blood, she felt alone and naked. One with the earth in confusion and fear. They sat under the tree for a long while and then Kalman helped her to her feet. They walked hand in hand through the woods. Once they reached town they stopped and looked at each other. They exchanged a light kiss and then both went their separate way. It was the last time Kalman would ever see her. In less than a month her entire family would disappear. Only the tree bore witness to their moment of togetherness. The tree and the ground into which her blood had soaked would always bear silent witness to their frailty and their strength and their naked humanness.

kielbasa

A black bird, its feathers reflecting a silvery metallic shimmer under the winter sun, grabbed at a piece of carrion from the frozen ground, while Chiel Willner broke into an abandoned farmhouse and snatched a piece of spoiled *kielbasa* lying on the kitchen counter to fend off the terrible gnawing hunger in his stomach.

It was the dead of winter, January, 1941, and Chiel was making his way back to Dombrowa after spending several weeks in the Montelupe prison in Krakow. The officer whose horses Chiel had been charged with taking care of was suspected of collaborating with a Jewish girl and had promptly disappeared from Pustkow. Chiel was taken into custody and questioned by the Gestapo as to the officer's whereabouts. When he was unable to answer their questions, he was promptly sent to the Montelupe Prison where he was beaten and tortured by the SS for weeks. Finally after failing to punch, kick and pry any information from him with fists, boots and pliers, Chiel was set free - bruised, battered and broken. Had he not been given traveling papers by the officer with the horses before he had gone off with the Jewish girl, Chiel would have never made it back to Dombrowa. As it were, he was able to pass checkpoints and traverse main roads without being stopped. He walked for days, often waist deep in snow with nothing but rags on his feet. The insulation from the snow kept his feet from freezing solid.

On the final evening of his journey, overcome with fatigue and hunger, with the last remnants of his energy being rapidly consumed by constant shivering, Chiel came upon the old farmhouse. He peered through the window. On the kitchen table sat plates and dishes of half-eaten food grown moldy with time. On the counter was a bowl of sour milk that had turned greenish-brown. A whisk and spoon still sat in the middle of the bowl. Chairs had been overturned and there were old papers strewn about the floor, as if whoever lived there had left in a great hurry in the middle of breakfast.

Chiel broke in through the window and grabbed a piece of *kielbasa* off the kitchen counter, tearing at it with his teeth like a starving dog. He swallowed whole chunks without so much as even chewing, and then continued on through the woods. Within an hour he had reached Dombrowa. It was early in the morning and he went straight to his house. The whole family was there to greet him, including Kalman. When Chiel stepped through the door his mother gasped. She knew it was her son, but beneath the dirt and blood and multi-colored bruises he looked like a corpse. She ran up and helped him inside. Kalman and Mr. Willner then helped him onto a small cot to rest. He had no longer lie down when he began to vomit profusely. Kalman watched as chunks of fetid *kielbasa* came pouring out of his brother's mouth, and he was afraid that his dear brother would surely die from food poisoning in his already weakened state.

But die, he did not. He lay in bed for a week and was nursed back to health by his mother and father. Even Moshe and Sarah helped. They put wet rags on his head, brought him water, helped to clean him up and get him back on his feet again. By the second week Chiel had gained enough strength to join Kalman at work.

gone

In the spring of '41 word was given by the Council
that each family must choose one member to work in a factory
in the village of Mielec.
Chiel volunteered to go.
His father was too sick and
Kalman, being the oldest,
would be better able to watch over the others.
A few short days later on
one overcast afternoon, Chiel was gone.
He never returned.

lineman

In May of the same year, the Jewish Council was instructed to find more men to work at Pustkow. Kalman was again selected. He feared that if the commandant remembered him and that he had escaped, he would surely be killed. Or worse. But to run or hide - to *not* go - meant his family would suffer the consequences. He had no choice but to revisit the work camp he had escaped from months earlier.

Upon his return, Kalman found that no one had remembered him except his friend, Ignac Stiglietz, who also hailed from Dombrowa. The guards were all new, as was the commandant, a sadistic bastard. Barbed wire now surrounded the camp. Guards were posted at the perimeter, armed with machine-guns and German Shepherds. An *appelplatz*, or meeting square, had been built in the center of the camp, and barracks assembled to house the prisoners, whose job it was to lay telephone lines

The routine was the same. The prisoners were woken up before sunrise and forced to gather in the *appelplatz* to be counted. Sometimes they would stand for fifteen minutes and sometimes for an hour or two. They could not move, bend over, go to the bathroom or talk. Just stand. Wind, rain or sun, they were to stand until the commandant had completed the count. If you had diarrhea or were sick and unable to stand, you would be beaten. If you soiled your pants you would be beaten and forced to wear the same pants throughout the day. There were no choices. There was no forgiveness.

After the count they would be given a thin soup or small crust of bread, never enough to satisfy the constant hunger, but just a taste of food, enough to keep them going until their next "meal". Then it was off to work.

Kalman's first job was to paint the bottom of the poles with a special tar before it was placed in the ground. The noxious fumes and toxic solvent from the tar soaked through his shoes, and at night his feet burned so badly that he was unable to sleep.

The guards saw that Kalman was a hard worker and soon he was promoted to wiring lamps on top of the poles. Dressed in their flimsy rags, the young men and boys would be led out through small villages and countryside laying telephone lines for the Reich. Outfitted with cheap clamps on his feet, Kalman shimmied up to the top of the pole and went about the task of wiring lamps. On warm, sunny days, with a light breeze blowing through the air, Kalman would often lean back and take a few extra minutes to do his work. Suspended twenty feet above ground, Kalman felt somewhat removed from his confinement and from the watchful eyes of the guards. He could rest for a moment, the hot sun on his face and cool breeze blowing through his air refreshing his spirit and giving him strength. But he was never too far removed from the guards, the SS, or the reality of his situation.

One afternoon early in June, a summer storm blew in with fierce winds and cold rain. Kalman had just finished wiring one line and was walking to the next when the storm hit. By the time he had reached the next pole, it had become as slippery as ice. Covered with a thin, slimy residue that had leached out of the wood, the pole was nearly impossible to climb. Kalman reached around the pole and clutched it tightly with his hands while hugging it as closely to his body as he could. He started to shimmy his way up, but before he was even a third of the way up, he slid back down. The guard was waiting for him at the bottom with a leather whip in his hand. As soon as Kalman reached the ground, the guard started lashing him with the whip, shouting, "Get up that pole you worthless pig!" The rain had soaked through his clothes, leaving his skin cold and damp, which made the crack of the leather whip sting like fire.

The guard continued lashing at Kalman with the whip and was joined by two other soldiers who were laughing and bolting out insults, "Come on monkey boy! Climb that pole!" they laughed. It was all a game to them, an amusement to break the dull routine. Finally Kalman gained enough of a grip to climb the pole and away from the whip and laughter. He was glad to be off of the ground in the relative nest of safety, but the wind and rain and cold were cutting through him, chilling him to the bone and causing him to shiver. His hands were growing slow and clumsy from the cold, and he had great difficulty manipulating the tools and wire. The guard below was yelling at him to hurry, and Kalman's head was pounding from lack of food.

Hanging atop the pole, Kalman could picture his mother on Sabbath. The challa bread and meat stew, the cinnamon and raisons, honey cake and sponge cake, all the family gathered in the warmness of their home, telling stories and sharing laughter, grandfather Kohane handing out little candies with a glint in his eye. All these things he remembered and for a moment he could feel himself back home with his family before the madness had begun. He yearned to be back home. To be with family and friends. He yearned for everything that had been lost. He yearned for the life he once had. Then he heard the caustic voice of his guard yelling at him and the memory broke like shattered glass.

"*Schnell! Schnell*! Be finished now!!" The guard yelled, growing increasingly inpatient in the rain. Kalman rubbed his hands together and blew hot breath into them, then hurriedly finished wiring the lamp. A gust of wind hit him, nearly toppling him over. To lose one's grip without a safety belt meant to break one's body. He managed to finish the wiring and began descending the pole when the winds again picked up. By the time he reached the ground, sheets of rain blew in with gale force winds. The guard was holding onto his helmet and wrapped in a black rain tarp. He stood at an angle into the wind to keep from toppling over. Kalman's skin was damp and raw from the frigid rain. His feet grew numb. When he landed on the ground, he felt electrical bolts jolt through his toes. The guard immediately stepped over to him. "*Schnell*! I said. Don't you hear with those Jewish ears of yours?" Then he shoved Kalman on the back, causing him to fall into the sloppy mud.

The other prisoners and guards had already packed up and were walking past Kalman, when a guard by the name of Sgt. Kieffer came upon him. Sgt. Kieffer stopped and pulled Kalman out of the slop. "Come, we must all hurry," he said.

Kalman looked up at Sgt. Kieffer, whose eyes were soft, expressing a compassion which he had not seen in many weeks.

daises

The following day brought back the sun, and the linemen were back out working. After several hours, they broke for lunch, which was always slightly better than the morning meal, but still not enough to fend off the constant hunger. As they were finishing their watery soup, Sgt. Kieffer stepped over to Kalman and threw his mess tin at him.

"Here boy, clean this for me."

Kalman did not look up, but simply grabbed the mess tin robotically, ready to just follow another order. He picked up the tin and was about to wipe it clean, when he noticed bits of potato and a small chuck of meat in the bottom of it. Kalman looked up at Kieffer, who then nodded his head up and down before stepping away.

Kalman hurriedly ate the meat and potatoes with his hands and then licked his fingers clean. It tasted better than all the feasts he had ever eaten. After that day Sgt. Kieffer had Kalman "clean" his tin often.

The days were getting longer as summer solstice approached. The Northern Hemisphere of the earth began its furthest tilt towards the sun and the feeling in camp grew more and more tense. Sgt. Kieffer approached Kalman one afternoon and told him, "Don't stray too far from the poles. That is all I can tell you."

On the very next day, a young boy was shot in a field no more than 50 meters from the pole he had been assigned to. Kalman learned later from his friend Ignac that the guards were given one week leave for shooting an escapee, two weeks for shooting two, and so on. Kalman was given the task of disposing of the body. He and a couple others loaded the boy's lifeless body into a wheelbarrow. The body was rigid from rigor mortis, and when they laid it into the wheelbarrow, the legs and arms remained fully extended, one arm cocked backwards, with the neck twisted off to one side. They pushed the wheelbarrow into the woods, dug a shallow grave with their hands and placed the body inside. *Dust to dust. Ashes to ashes.* It was as if the boy had never existed, except to Kalman and the others who buried him.

"What was his name? Do you know?" one of the boys asked.

"Issak. I think."

"And his last name?"

"Who has a last name in this damned place? We have no names." Another replied.

Kalman thought of the dead boy's family. They would never know what happened to their son. That is, if they themselves were still alive.

The boys then filled the grave back up with dirt, each scoop of soil making a sick "thud" when it hit the body. The two guards who had accompanied them into the woods had been dawdling in the distance, enjoying a cigarette and talking about the women they were screwing, when they grew inpatient and came up to gather the boys.

"You're done now. Let the wolves have the rest of him," the short, stocky one told them.

"Or water him, maybe he'll sprout daises," the other one laughed.

The boys stood up, gathered the wheelbarrow, and headed back to camp.

untermenschen

One June 22nd, 1941, the second day of summer, Germany launched *Barbarossa*, the massive offensive against Russia. In and outside of camp a flurry of activity was taking place. Massive lines of troops and armor were moving forward. Tempers grew short, and the sadistic commandant grew ever more volatile. Beatings and hangings were commonplace.

"Order must be kept at all costs," the commandant told the group of exhausted prisoners one afternoon as they stood in the *appelplatz.* A young boy, no older than thirteen, was drug out into the middle of the square by two soldiers.

"This pig was caught trying to escape. Do you know what happens to those who try to escape?"

Terror filled the boy's brown eyes. His eyes and lips were bloody and swollen.

"Let me demonstrate. Watch very carefully. If anyone is caught looking away from this pig then it will be his turn."

The boy was stripped naked and tied to a post. The commandant then produced a razor-laced whip and began to thrash the boy on his buttocks. The boy's screams pierced the afternoon sky and caused one's blood to run cold. The commandant continued whipping the boy until his buttocks became like ground beef. Finally the boy stopped screaming and passed out from the pain. Flies buzzed around his exposed gluteal muscles as he slumped from the pole.

Two Wehrmacht officers were standing on a hillside overlooking the camp and witnessed the entire episode. They immediately drove down to the camp and approached the commandant.

"What are you doing, man?" One officer demanded to know, a large, strapping man with a heavy mustache and deep voice.

"Have you gone mad? This is only a boy!"

The commandant, who was still dripping with sweat from his beat red face, did not even flinch when replying, "I am keeping order."

"Order, do you call whipping a young boy to near death keeping order?"

The group of prisoners who had been forced to witness the horrific scene was now shuffled away by guards as the Wehrmacht officers and the commandant continued to argue.

"This is insane!" the officers barked. "Who gave such an order to treat these prisoners like animals?"

"Our orders come directly from Reichsfurer Himmler. We are to use whatever means necessary to handle the *untermenschen*, the sub-humans. Perhaps you should take it up with Himmler," the SS commandant replied.

That was the last thing Kalman heard. By the time they had made it back to the barracks, the jeep with the two officers was driving out of Pustkow. Kalman's stomach sunk when he watched the jeep exit the gates. If a regular German officer could not help them, no one could. They were doomed. The SS had supremacy over all others, and the SS meant only one thing. Death.

escaping the spider's web

"Word is that one of the guards has it in for you Kalman," Ignac Stiglietz told his friend. "Be careful. You know how they are."

Kalman knew exactly how they were. And he also knew that if a guard had it in for you he would find a reason to act on it. No questions asked. After the morning meal, the prisoners were herded back out into the fields to line more poles. There were fewer soldiers to guard them as many were pulled to the front line. It was a warm, breezeless day and Kalman's hunger was constant and painful. Since the Russian offensive had broken out, rations were becoming ever more meager. If not for some Polish farmers who had risked their own lives to toss a potato or piece of bread at the prisoners when the guards weren't watching, they would surely have starved.

Kalman finished lining one lamp and descended the pole. The guards were standing near the top of a hillside overlooking the field when Kalman began walking to the next pole. On one side of the field was a forest. Kalman looked over his shoulder at the guards who were busy talking and laughing. Suddenly, Kalman veered off the path to the next pole and started heading towards the woods, which was approximately 25-30 meters away. Each meter felt like a mile. Kalman increased his stride. He quickly turned to look at the guards who were still standing on the hillside engaged in chatter. Kalman quickened his pace and held his breath as he hurried toward the woods. His body felt rigid and stiff and would not move fast enough. He felt eyes on him, eyes that would capture him. It was already too late to turn back, he was too far from the poles and Sgt. Kieffer's voice rang out in his head, "Don't walk too far from the poles."

In what seemed like an eternity, Kalman finally made it to the edge of the forest and began running. Dry branches and leaves cracked under his feet which alerted the guards. Gunfire rang out as Kalman continued to run, jumping over logs, fallen branches and gullies. The gunshots continued until finally Kalman was deep into the woods, and the firing weapons faded. He ran throughout the night. The woods were as dark as a deep cave. Owls and hawks hooted and screeched in the treetops. His shoes had fallen off in the commotion and his feet were bloodied and blistered from the sharp twigs and rocks.

In the pre-dawn hours as the temperature began to drop, weakened by fatigue and hunger, Kalman began to chill. A coldness which wrapped itself around the core of his body caused him to shiver violently, nearly stealing his breath away with each forceful muscle contraction. He had made it through the forest and now found himself on the edge of a large wheat field. He walked 10 or 15 meters into the field and lay down, covering himself with wheat stocks for warmth. He dozed off briefly until the sun rose and the birds began chirping. He ate some raw wheat to fend off the gnawing emptiness in his stomach, and then slowly headed out of the field towards a small red barn. No one was in the barnyard so he carefully stepped into the barn and found some hens. As soon as the old hens saw Kalman they started clucking loudly. Kalman shooed them away and grabbed a couple of raw eggs, then ran out of the barn before the hens woke the farmer. After he cleared the barnyard and field, he hid behind a tree, wiped the white feathers and chicken shit off the shells, and tossed the raw eggs down his throat in one slimy gulp.

At the end of the second day, Kalman reached the Vistula, the largest river in Poland. He followed the riverbank up and down for hours looking for a crossing but to no avail. He considered swimming across, but it was too wide and too swift and he would surely drown. After several hours of searching, he came across a bridge. There was only one problem. The Germans were guarding it.

With nowhere else to go but across the bridge, Kalman grabbed his *motec*, a shovel-like tool used for digging potatoes which he had found in a field, and started walking toward the bridge. His only hope was that the two soldiers on the bridge would think he was a farmer. As he got closer, Kalman could hear the footsteps from heavy boots on the wooden platform as the guards walked across it. There was one on each end of the bridge and they walked back and forth continuously, passing each other in the middle. By the time Kalman reached the edge of the river, his heart was beating so fast and loud that he thought the guards would hear it through his chest.

One of the guards saw Kalman approaching and stopped to look at him. Kalman glanced at the soldier, nodded, and kept walking. When he stepped onto the bridge and passed the soldier, Kalman felt his heart pounding through his chest. "They'll hear me, they'll hear my heart," he kept thinking over and over. The young soldier watched Kalman as he passed, and then continued marching to the end of the bridge. Kalman never looked back and continued to the opposite end where he met the second soldier. As he got closer his anxiety was so great that he wanted to run, to run as fast as he possibly could, but he managed to maintain a slow, steady pace. Finally, he approached the second guard. Sweat poured off his forehead. His heart pounded. The next thing he knew he was stepping off the bridge onto solid ground. The second guard had barely even acknowledged him. He was free!

As he scurried away from the bridge and the guards and Pustkow, Kalman gasped for breath. He realized he hadn't even breathed since stepping onto the bridge. Once clear from the sight of the soldiers, he started running until he reached a small village. There were still some Jewish stores open in this district of Poland. Kalman found a small hardware store and stepped inside. The owner of the store, a small, middle aged Jewish fellow, knew right away that Kalman had escaped from Pustkow. He gave Kalman a bite to eat and told him which direction he needed to go.

For two days Kalman followed dirt roads on the way back to Dombrowa. He hitched-hiked rides from farmers on horse-driven wagons, slept in a hay pile in an empty barn, found more eggs to eat, until finally he was back home in Dombrowa. Again he went to his Uncle Shilek's place to hide. One of his cousins ran into town and told his mother and father that Kalman was back, and they immediately came running over to see him.

For the moment he was safe and back with his family, except for Chiel, whom no one had heard from.

Ignac Stiegletz was questioned for two days as to the whereabouts of his friend Kalman. Ignac may well have saved Kalman's life by telling them he had gone the opposite direction of where he actually went.

Kalman had escaped the spider's web, but remained in the wolf's den, and the wolves were becoming increasingly rabid as all of Europe descended further into bloodshed, fire and madness.

Chapter 7

Prayers, bats and manure

K alman awoke in the early morning hours upon his return to Dombrowa in the attic of uncle Shilek's house. He had been dreaming of his baby sister Sarah. He and Chiel were pushing her down the road in a stroller. Kalman could see her curly hair bouncing up and down and she was singing an old song with the voice of an angel. The birds in the trees were singing with her and the two brothers were laughing and running with the stroller toward their house where mama was waiting with fresh bread and honey cake.

Lying with his head on the pillow, his eyes closed, Kalman felt himself still in the dream. A feeling of happiness spread through his body and for a moment he looked forward to the day ahead of him. Then reality overtook him and a deep, sinking feeling hit his stomach like hot lead - a sickening, anxious swirling that began in his gut and spread through his body like fiery ice. He lay frozen for a moment and then stoically rose from bed and ventured downstairs to face the day. The only awakening from this nightmare would be liberation by the Red Army. That was their hope. If they could hold out one more day, perhaps that would be the day they would be set free.

For several weeks Kalman stayed in Dombrowa. By day he worked in the village of Shkenca under the auspices of the Jewish Council and visited his family in the evening as circumstances allowed. On most days the village was patrolled by the Jewish Police with a scattering of Brown Shirts, and everything was relatively quiet, but that would quickly change upon the arrival of the SS, which was becoming ever more frequent. The Gestapo would arrive in town and demand money, men, or both; and were becoming increasingly barbaric.

The men of the SS were seen as visitors from hell, demons sent to bring pain and suffering to the earth; but these were not demons, they were *men*. They were fathers and sons and brothers - and they were cruel and sadistic and void of compassion. They were human beings and humans were supposed to have been

created in the image of God. So if man was capable of such evil –
then what of God? Or of man's *image* of God?

Moshe and Sarah had lost so much weight that Kalman could
see the bony outline of their eye sockets, which were made even
more prominent by the dark circles under their eyes. Sarah's knees
began to bow from lack of nutrients and resembled two knobby
stubs on skinny sticks. Her hair, which had always been thick and
shiny, began to grow dull and thin. Kalman's mother carried an
anguished look on her emaciated face, while his father, burdened
with worry and grief, stricken by severe stomach cramps, seemed to
grow old before Kalman's eyes.

To witness his family endure so much was often more than
Kalman could bear, and his father's words added much confusion
and despair to it all.

"God is punishing us," his father would repeat over and over
with a sense of despairing resignation. "How could a man have so
much power as Hitler unless he was sent by God to punish us for
our sins?"

If God had his hand in this, Kalman thought, then we truly
are in hell. He did not know what to think or what to believe. All
he could do was hope that it would end and that his family would be
spared. He was no more than a worthless parasite in the eyes of the
Reich, but he knew he was loved and that love was keeping him
alive.

For six weeks Kalman worked for a Polish farmer along with a
wealthy Jewish couple from Krakow who had paid their way into
the job along with their daughter and sister-in-law. Kalman fed the
pigs and cows. He fertilized fields where he honed the fine

technique of pitching manure with a five pronged pitchfork. Without the proper elbow and wrist technique - a twist here and a pitch there - the horse dung would drop to the ground and back into the pile before he could spread it out onto the fields. Kalman became a master pitcher and it would serve him well. The farmer was also a small time beekeeper and Kalman helped tend to the buzzing orange hive.

While the farmer was outfitted with a mesh mask and smoke pump, Kalman had only loose trousers, an oversized shirt and old shoes with no socks to protect his pale skin. The bees flew up his pants and down his shirt and left welts on him until he started to look like a swollen Buddha. He devised strategies to deal with the bees, including tying strings around his ankles to keep them out of his loose pants, and after a couple of weeks, his body grew immune to the stings. Eventually he learned that if you didn't disturb them, went about your task slowly and deliberately, and were careful not to stir them up, the bees would generally leave you alone. The bees were not so unlike the Germans, except the Germans were much more unpredictable and their stings were usually fatal.

On the sixth week the mayor of Skrzynka issued a directive that no Jews were allowed to work and Kalman was sent back to Dombrowa. While returning home Kalman sensed a change in the village. Approaching the outskirts of town near the edge of the woods, he noticed everything was very quiet. Too quiet. Like an animal that has an innate sense of danger, Kalman too had developed a special acuity for suspicious activity. He stayed hidden in the woods and listened. From the center of town came echoes of barking dogs, the shouting of men and muffled cries. Then he heard shots ring out. What he could not see was the scene unfolding in the Market Square. The Gestapo had arrived in town early in the morning shortly after Kalman had left for the farm. They gathered up forty to fifty men, women and children and brought them to the square where they were forced to kneel on the hot cobblestone with their heads hung low. Anyone caught raising their head up would be shot. A few of the elderly simply collapsed from heat stroke and died on the spot, while others, knees blistered from the constant pressure of the bricks, their legs and backs cramping terribly from the static position they were forced to hold, could not endure it any longer and tried to shift positions and were promptly shot.

When Kalman heard the shots, he thought of only one thing. His family. Terrified that they were trapped inside with no way to escape, Kalman made his way to the *parobik*. A *parobik* is a cattle wrangler of sorts, and Kalman knew one who had worked for his father for many years. He lived in a tiny wooden shack in the woods with his wife and nine children. He would know what happened to Kalman's family.

As he made his way to the shack, Kalman was haunted by images of his family. Were they scared? What was happening to them? Were they suffering? Perhaps even dead....then what? He could not go on without his family. The world would be nothing more than an empty ball of clay without his family. It would not be worth living upon. Kalman tried to force the images out of his mind until he reached the shack. He knocked on the rickety door and one of the children answered. The child resembled a small urchin. Kalman immediately stepped inside and approached the *parobik*, "Where are my parents?" He pleaded. "Have you seen them? What is happening?"

The *parobik*, a thin, wiry man with powerful, stringy arms, a week old beard and dark black eyes the shade of charcoal, a man who looked to have been anywhere from forty to eighty years old, walked over to Kalman and placed his hand on the young boy's shoulder. "They're safe Kalman. They escaped to the woods before the action started."

Kalman was so relieved by these words he nearly fell to the floor. The *parobik* then gave him directions as to where they may have fled. Kalman ran into the woods as fast as he could until he reached the spot where the *parobik* said his family had gone. He lie down on the ground and began shouting; "Tata! Tata!" On the ground he figured the sound would carry better through the forest. For over an hour he called out until at last he heard footsteps approaching. The sound of leaves and branches cracked as the footsteps grew nearer. Then he heard the most wonderful sound in the world, a voice from the heavens. "Kalman, is that you?" His father's voice rang out. "Kalman?"

"Tata! It is I! Tata, I am here!"

They quickly ran to each other. Kalman could feel the moisture of his father's tears on his shoulder as they embraced.

"Come Kalman, we have found a safe spot."

Father and son walked deeper into the woods until they came upon a large pit surrounded by thick foliage. From the pit came soulful prayers from the deep voice of uncle Shlomo Kohane, a rabbi from Krakow and Kalman's maternal uncle.

It was Yom Kippur eve. Standing in the pit and hidden from the world by a web of trees were Kalman's mother, sister Sarah and brother Moshe, along with aunts and uncles and cousins. They were offering the *Vidui* – the confession of sins – on this Day of Atonement. Rabbi Kohane was wearing a *kittel*, a white robe in which the dead are buried and also worn for special ceremonies; and through him the family was offering their prayers of forgiveness for sins committed against God during the previous year.

On this day deep in the woods on the holiest of holy days, the Sabbath of Sabbaths, this beleaguered family gathered under the stars and the moon and offered their deepest prayers unto God, and though Kalman could not for the life of him imagine what sins *they* could have committed amidst all the horror afflicted upon them, he felt that it was through his family and their prayers in which God dwelled, and that He was in the midst of their suffering.

From deep within him rose a sense of deep spiritual connection *and* disgust. One thing he did know, however, was that he was deeply grateful for being back with his family, yet he didn't know if he should offer thanks to God, or perhaps to the trees for hiding them.

But philosophical inquires had no place in the shadow of a pit in a thicket of woods in an occupied land where you are considered no more than a louse who must be exterminated. Hans Frank, Governor-General of the Occupied Polish Territories based in Krakow, made this perfectly clear in his speeches "Gentlemen, I must ask you to rid yourselves of all feeling of pity. We must annihilate the Jews, wherever we find them and wherever it is possible. Jews and lice must be exterminated; even the lice on Jews must be annihilated."

And each time Uncle Rabbi Shlomo Kohane pounded his chest, repeating, *"Al Cheit! Al Cheit!"* I sin! I sin! Kalman feared who may be listening in the shadows. For fear was his constant companion. Fear which superseded all else. Fear which reeked in his sweat as he walked down an empty road. Fear which stuck on his hands and fingers as he ate a raw egg. Fear which made a rainbow after a summer rain vanish before his eyes. Fear which rendered invisible the beauty of a sunset or the blossoming of a flower. And now, fear of who may discover his family gathered in the pit, and pounce as a leopard on a rabbit den.

Only one thing came into the pit to hear them this cool summer night as the prayers turned from Atonement to Pleading, as Rabbi Kohane and Kalman's father cried out into the woods, pleading with their hearts, "God, where are you? Why do you make us suffer so? Why have you brought such evil into the world?" The only thing that answered them as Rabbi Kohane pounded on his chest was a bat which had swooped down from the tree top, nearly clipping Kalman on the shoulder with its wings as it veered off at a sharp angle and disappeared into the night.

Only the bat had heard their prayers.

As the night grew colder and the prayers complete, the family walked together to an empty barn which belonged to a farmer Kalman's father had befriended years earlier, and they curled together in a hayloft to keep warm.

Kalman slept with one eye open.

a safer place

Early the next morning the farmer met Kalman's father outside of the barn and Kalman could hear their muffled voices as they spoke.

"Herschl, I would let you stay, you know that I would, but I can't. The Germans have been crawling all over these woods. They were here just two days ago. Herschl - I have a family, if they catch you here we're all dead. I have a cellar where one or two people could stay, but you know the Gestapo, they smell cellars out like the dogs they are."

Mr. Willner was answering the farmer but Kalman could out make out what he was saying. In a couple of minutes his father came back into the barn, and Kalman pretended to be sleeping.

"Everyone must get up," his father spoke. "We cannot stay here any longer and Dombrowa is not safe. We must find a safer place. Somewhere where we may be allowed to work."

Then he pulled Kalman aside and pulled a piece of fabric out of his rucksack and gave it to him. It was a piece of fine gabardine.

"Kalman, I want you to take this. You speak perfect Polish, go find a farm, make up a story that you are an orphan, offer them the fabric and perhaps they will allow you to stay and work for them. It is not good to stay with us."

Kalman desperately wanted to stay with his family, but after seeing the care and concern in his father's eyes, he couldn't argue with him, it would just bring more pain to the family.

"Don't worry," his parents told him. "We'll meet up in a safer place. Now you must go."

Kalman walked for the better part of the day until he reached a small farm. He thought of his family standing in the barn where he left them. The look of sorrow etched into his mother's face. The bewilderment of Sarah and Moshe. How could a three or a six year old child understand such madness? But before he could reflect any further a dog started barking. Kalman froze and his skinny muscles became as rigid as cable wires.

Ever since he had been chased in the woods two winters ago by a soldier's German Shepherd, the mere sight of a dog evoked a surge of pure adrenaline. It was on a cold, bitter day when an SS guard caught sight of Kalman walking along the edge of the woods. It was past curfew and to be caught meant a bullet. Kalman easily outran the soldier, but not before he had unleashed his dog. The brown and black Shepherd seemed to have flown over the snow in long, smooth leaps, easily catching up to Kalman and knocking him to the ground with ninety pounds of thick, coarse fur, claws and gnashing fangs. The German Shepherd was biting down on his leg when Kalman managed to roll over and pull a large bread knife out of his boot. He plunged the blade into the dog over and over until the raging dog grew limp and its powerful jaws released Kalman's leg. As if in a trance of fury and terror, Kalman kept tearing at the dog, finally ripping its stomach open and pulling out the intestines until the snow was stained in blood and the animal's viscera was strewn about in piles of shiny blue and red entrails. When he got back home he was covered head to toe with blood, the dog's and his own, and it had frozen solid onto his hair and nostrils. His mother nearly passed out when she saw him walking through the door.

The farmer's dog barked again and Kalman was ready to reach for the knife when the farmer came out of the house and called the dog off.

"Son, what are you doing out here?" The farmer called out.

"I'm looking for work,, sir. Don't want any money – just food and a place to stay."

The farmer looked Kalman over.

"I have something," Kalman said as he reached into his bag and pulled out the fabric. "It's good fabric, sir; it's yours if you want it."

The farmer continued looking at Kalman.

"Son, I wish I could help you but I can't. You're on the run, I know that. I'm sorry but I can't help you. You're welcome to stay the night but I can't chance it after that."

Kalman felt like a contagious disease that no one wanted to catch.

"I understand sir."

He stayed the night in an empty shed. In the morning the farmer gave him a loaf of bread and hunk of cheese. "I'm really very sorry, boy, but these are terrible times and I can't risk my family. You go ahead and keep that fabric, it may come in handy."

And that was that. Kalman was back on the road.

Not knowing which way to turn, Kalman decided to cross the Vistula once again and head to Stobnica, a filthy little town that sat in another district and was still more open than the Krakow district under Governor Frank. In Stobnica the Jew's were still allowed to work and Kalman hoped it would be easier for him to find someone willing to hire him.

When he arrived in the village Kalman discovered that his entire family was also there. His father had told him they would meet again, but never did Kalman imagine it would be so soon and he was overwhelmed with joy. It seemed a miracle. But all was not as he hoped it would be. There was no work to be found anywhere, not for him or anyone else. There was nothing to do but pass time during the day as the minutes and hours lingered endlessly. Stobnica was still in the Middle Ages and had no plumbing, no toilets, not even an outhouse. There was garbage strewn about the village and piles of human waste scattered everywhere. During the day they were forced to stay on the outskirts of town in an open field. Not far from them was a ditch which was used as an open sewer and a foul odor permeated the air making everyone nauseated. At night the Jews in town snuck them in to sleep in their hallways or sheds.

Kalman had only been there for two to three days when his father again told him to go out and find work elsewhere. "Just speak Polish and no one will ever know," he told him.

No one would know, that is, as long as he kept his pants on. Only Jewish men were circumcised in Poland those days. So again Kalman left his family behind and set out to find work and to stay alive.

to be somewhere

After several rejections, Kalman found a farmer with twelve acres of land, two horses, six cows, a few pigs and some chickens. Kalman told him he had lost his family and needed work, not for money, just for food and a place to stay. The farmer, a large, rotund man with a perpetually sunburned face, a pug nose and thin, scraggly hair, agreed to let Kalman try out for the job.

"Let me see what you can do," he told Kalman gruffly while throwing him a pitchfork.   Luckily Kalman had experience and went about unloading a pile of manure from a wagon and spreading it onto the field.

"Good work, boy!   You can stay in the barn.   We have breakfast at sunup and supper at sundown."

"Yes sir," Kalman answered.

"Jacek!" the farmer called out.   "Come show Karol where he can sleep."

Jacek was a Polish boy in his early teens.   He had a pale complexion, dull eyes and bushy eyebrows.   His neck was long and thin and a huge Adam's apple stuck out from the middle of it. Kalman thought his barn-mate looked like he swallowed an egg.

The following day Kalman arose before the roosters, mainly because the hay was sticking up through a hole in his pants and he was dreaming a roach was making a nest in his butt.   He went outside to a water spigot, took the handle and gave it a couple pumps, splashed some water on his face and then drank for two minutes.   The road had made him parched and he could feel the water replenishing his body and spirit as he drank.   Feeling somewhat refreshed, he made his way over to the main house where the farmer and his wife were already up.

Soon the whole household was awake, the three young daughters and three sons joined in for a light breakfast along with Kalman and Jacek.   Once the sun had risen over the horizon, the work began - feeding the chickens, cows and pigs - cleaning the horses, fertilizing the fields, mending fence, whatever needed done. At noon they would break for lunch, usually a big loaf of bread with cheese and a huge bowl of soup.   They worked from dusk to dawn and then all gathered in the main house for dinner. Everyone ate out of the same bowl with large wooden spoons; soup, stew, sometimes a piece of beef or chicken, lots of cabbage and potatoes, carrots and beets.

The hard, honest work coupled with hearty meals and plenty of fresh well-water had put some meat on Kalman's bones and he began to fill out somewhat. His clothes smelled of horses and cows and wheat and it was a far cry better than the fetid conditions in Stobnice. At night, fatigued from the day – but a fatigue which was healthy and natural– Kalman was asleep as soon as he plopped onto the straw, which was now covered with a thick cotton blanket, and his last thoughts of the day were always the same as they were upon awakening, thoughts of his family. When sitting at the dinner table with the Polish family, he yearned for his own family. He could still smell his mother's cooking and the wonderful, warm feeling of the Sabbath when all the worries of the world would disappear for the day. Those times now seemed like a distant dream.

Kalman worked at the farm for nearly a month and a half, when one morning before breakfast the farmer pulled him aside.

"Karol, you not Polish are you?"

Kalman said nothing. He wanted to run. To hide.

"You friend Jacek heard you speaking Yiddish in dreams last night whilst you sleeping. No Polish boys I know speak Yiddish."

Kalman stood silent, afraid of what the farmer might do.

"Boy," the farmer continued. "We all like you here, but I have family, six children, a farm. Do you know what would happen? I can't risk family's life. I tell you what I do. My sister live 6 km from here. A widow with one child. She hire you."

The farmer gave Kalman a loaf of bread and some turnips and sent him off. Kalman could see Jacek sitting at the kitchen table. "Some friend," Kalman mumbled to himself.

He walked down the country road past old stone barns, sat next to a small pond grown stagnant with greenish-brown algae and watched water bugs skim across the surface as he chewed on sour bread and cheese. He was already hungry and the familiar gnawing in his stomach had returned. It was noon time and his thoughts turned to the thick soup being served at the farmer's house and he was overcome with loneliness.

Then Kalman heard a truck rounding the corner of the road. It sounded like the troop carriers which had brought death to Dombrowa and to Grandmother Willner two years earlier. He jumped up and ran behind an old stone wall, dropping his bread in the scummy water in haste. The truck grew nearer. Kalman held his breath as it passed in front of the wall. He stared at a weed growing out from a crack between the mortar and stone as the truck drove down the road. Once it was a distance down the road, Kalman peeked his head up. It was as old, beat up truck full of chickens on their way to slaughter.

Kalman leaned against the wall in repose, his energy spent, and it hit him. He was alone. He was a rabbit in a wolf's den. There was nowhere to hide. Nowhere to run. No one to help him. He was hungry, tired and thirsty. He wanted to sleep. He wanted to be somewhere, but he was nowhere. Everywhere was nowhere. His family could well be dead. Dombrowa could be dead. His whole world could be dead.

He wanted to be *somewhere*.

That evening he slept in a corn field. The moon was just a shadow, its round fullness a dull, gray orb, the bottom a curl of silvery-white. It looked like a gray pumpkin with a smile. Kalman wished he were sitting on it.

The next day he continued up the road until he reached the farmer's sister's house. She had one cow, two acres of rocky land and a young daughter. She could not keep Kalman.

"A widow with a young girl – if they found you here, we would be killed."

Kalman heard her answer even before the words left her lips.

He was allowed to stay the night. In the morning he was given a few eggs, some bread, and he was gone.

There was only one place to go now.

Dombrowa.

Even if he were killed, at least it would be while trying to go home.

Home.

Whatever that may be.

Chapter 8

the cracker box

*H*ome. *I must get home.*

Every step of Kalman's swollen feet brought him closer. But to what?

And to whom?

His mind raced through a tangled web of disparate images and scattered emotions. Distant memories of laughter and play danced with melting candy, sticky pants pockets and the old Synagogue; along with his father's broad shoulders as they marched down the street to avenge for Kalman's split ear. Memories of blueberries and cinnamon; headless chickens and cold nights spent in the warmth of their small house, gathered around the crackling wood stove as Grandmother Willner lie in the corner. Reflections of his mother's beloved mama and papa, Labish and Chana Beila Kohane, the gentlest of spirits.

What great joy! And his heart sang.

BUT NOW???? And as if from a lighting bolt the fond memories were seared from his breast, fading as distant thunder, leaving only the rumbling of sadness and fear in its wake. Fear of what may be awaiting him at home.

They're gone! Gone! He cried out as cursed visions flooded his mind.

Grandmother Willner lying in a puddle of blood – dear old Grandfather – beard ripping – crying out for help – gunshots – blood.............

NO! Will not think – Can not think - NO – Not real – Get home – Home – HOME!

Kalman plodded on, step by step, until he reached the confines of Dombrowa.

It was 3:00 in the afternoon and a faint breeze blew across his face.

What Kalman saw was a village transformed. A tiny section of town had been quarantined with a hastily made wall that encircled a group of old, dilapidated shacks. On one side was wire and fence and on the other, behind the shacks, a partition made of old, wooden planks nailed together like a poorly constructed jigsaw puzzle. It resembled one of the pig pens Kalman shoveled shit in, but Kalman knew this was no pig pen. It was a ghetto. If his family were still alive, this is where they would be.

The streets were nearly empty and no Germans were around, so Kalman snuck into town and ran to the cemetery where he could see the main gate leading into the ghetto. Standing guard at the gate was Shimek, a friend of Kalman's who was wearing the uniform of the Jewish Police. Kalman edged closer to the fence and called out to his friend. "Shimek, it's Kalman, Kalman Willner."

Shimek held his Billy club tightly, smacking it down into his hand with a loud slap.

"Who is that? What do you want?"

Shimek fists blanched red and white from gripping the stick so tightly.

"Come out where I can see you!" he ordered.

"Shimek, it is I," Kalman answered as he stepped out in front of the gate.

"Kalman, what are you doing here?" Shimek asked, loosening his grip on the stick.

"Let me in."

"You want *in* this place? Are you mad? Look around you."

People were milling about the ghetto in tattered clothes. The women wearing thick, black stockings, gray overcoats, many with scarves wrapped around their heads. The men in traditional black pants and jackets, but worn and dusty, as if the clothes they wore were the only ones they had left. Some women were holding young children who looked like rag dolls, lethargic and dazed from lack of food. One young girl held a doll in her hand, and though she looked weary, she still had a smile on her face as she coddled her porcelain playmate. Kalman nearly cried when he looked at the young girl.

"Sarah," he thought out loud. "Shimek, my family? Are they here?"

"I haven't seen them, Kalman, but today is my first day. You're welcome to come in and look, but you better hurry before they see you. If you get caught without papers or orders you'll be shot."

Kalman passed through the gate. On one side was the *vanna*, the bathhouse where he and his father and uncles and grandfather had bathed and steamed. It was dry now and overgrown with weeds. On the other was the largest building in town. It had belonged to his friend Shlek's father, Mr. Schindler, the grain dealer.

The last time he saw Shiek was when they were walking down the street with Chiel, when Kalman thought he had seen the ghosts of Rabbi's making their way toward the Synagogue. Shiek had said, "The only ghosts around here are us. We're gonna be the ghosts – all of us." A cold chill ran down Kalman's spine.

Shindler's building was used by the Gestapo now. He was gunned down in the market square along with the other leaders of town on the first day of the occupation. Shiek and his mother were murdered while lying in their beds on the same day.

Kalman stepped through the gate of the ghetto and immediately met some friends of the family. Kalman knew practically everyone in the village, having lived there his whole life, and it was only a few minutes before he discovered that his family was in the ghetto.

"They're at the Rand house," he was told by an orthodox Hasid, the sweat dripping off his long, black beard. The Rand home was a small, unassuming, wooden cracker box which barely housed one family. Now it was home to nine. Nine families squeezed into one room. Kalman rushed over to the house and found his parents, along with Moshe and Sarah, sitting on the front porch. Mrs. Willner cupped her hands under her chin and cried out, "It's a miracle! God in heaven it's a miracle! My Kalman is alive!"

Sarah and Moshe walked up slowly and hugged their big brother, while Mr. Willner stood at the porch clutching his chest, his eyes beaming with pride and joy as he watched his son. Kalman walked up to greet his parents, with Moshe and Sarah at his side.

"I knew you would come back to us, Kalman," his father told him. "I could feel it in my heart."

"Kalman," his mother cried. "When you left us in Stobnica, I thought I would never see you again. My boy, my oldest son, a man, I could not bear to lose you again."

"I'm here, mama. I won't go away ever again," Kalman replied, wrapping his arms around her and giving her a soft kiss. "Ever again."

puddles of breath

The next morning Kalman was sent to work with a group of 100 to 150 other men by the Jewish Council. They were all put in wagons and carted off to the work sites. Whatever drudgery the Germans needed done, the men and boys from the ghetto were the ones to do it. From dusk to dawn Kalman worked outside the ghetto, returning at night to eat a meager meal, and then join his family at the Rand house.

At night the small house was stacked with living, breathing bodies. Nine families in one small shack. Kalman felt like he was living in the midst of a human bee hive; a cluster of men, women, children and crying babies beneath one roof. There was one bed with a mother, father and two children in it. As for the others, it was the floor, lying shoulder to shoulder with someone at their feet and someone's feet in their face. The air in the room was sticky and stagnant, the expelled breath from so many lungs causing the windows to fog up. In the morning as the air became cooler, the fog condensed, forming droplets which streamed down the window and dripped onto the floor into a small puddle of human breath.

They shared the floor with spiders, mites, and an occasional cockroach or snake. Whenever anyone had to relieve themselves they must step over and through a mound of people to get out. But usually it was *on* someone else; a human rug under one's feet, each step falling softly onto a belly or hard onto a shin bone and always eliciting the same response - a curse or a grunt. "Watch out! What are you doing?" Or a cry or a whimper.

The ghetto was guarded by the Jewish Police. The SS came into town occasionally from Tarnow, but didn't bother themselves much with the ghetto. They understood as well as the prisoners did; "Where would they hide? Where could they go?"
A German sergeant and two underlings passed by the fence one evening, stopping at the gate to amuse themselves. The sergeant was a thin, rat-like man with no chin and beady little eyes.

"This, gentleman," he said in a rather high pitch, feminine voice, "is our zoo. Ugly little creatures they are. I would only hope that more would try to escape, I need the target practice." As he spoke his two companions laughed mindlessly, the alcohol in their blood heightening their stupidity.

"Yeah sergeant, but some of these women would be good for a night if only they would clean themselves like real human beings."

"Oh," the sergeant sneered. "We have that under control. The finer of the beasts are in different cages," he sneered. Then the three goons continued walking down the street towards the pub, laughing all the way.

The Gestapo would carry out whatever business was at hand; random shootings, violent arrests and assaults, beatings, and then go to a pub down the street to drink before returning to Tarnow. Often the sounds of their revelry; laughter, German marching sounds and the clank of glasses could be heard through the night air as the families huddled within their cramped tombs.

bartering with memories

Before sunrise the able bodied men and boys of the camp were marched through the gate and utilized as human mules; digging trenches, carrying bricks, plowing fields and harvesting wheat and vegetables for the German army. Food in the ghetto, however, was scarce and often nonexistent.

"We must get food," Mrs. Willner told her husband. "How can we live without food? What are we to do? Eat the rats?"

"And where do we get this food?" Mr. Willner gently replied. "There is nothing but weeds in this cursed place."

"But the Poles have food, the peasants, surely they would…"

"And the peasants eat it," Mr. Willner interjected before his wife could finish.

Sarah was sitting in the corner and spoke not a word. Mr. Willner looked over at his baby girl. She seemed so sad, so vulnerable. She had no anger. No blame. No spite. She didn't ask why or how. She knew only that she was hungry. Mr. Willner, in his grief, began to wail, to scream and cry unto the heavens; to berate himself mercifully for not being able to feed and to protect his sweet, trusting child, but his screams and cries were silent, locked within himself where no one could hear them and no one could see them.

"There is a way," he uttered, answering his wife and himself, speaking to no one and to everyone.

"Kalman," his father said that evening. "The peasants are always milling about at night. I have spoken to others who have traded with them for food."

"But what can we trade papa? We have nothing here."

"Grandmother's house is right across the street. The house has been ransacked but surely there must be something left. We must get in there. I have found a hole in the fence, tonight we will go."

That night while the camp was sleeping, Kalman and his father slipped out of the house. Behind it was the wooden fence. As his father watched for guards, Kalman crawled out of the ghetto through a loose board in the fence and ran across the street to his grandmother and grandfather Kohane's place.

He found a broken window in the back and hurried inside, cutting his leg on a jagged piece of glass. The house was in shambles, all the silver, jewelry, family heirlooms, even picture frames had been taken by the Germans. What was left of their meager furniture was turned over, broken, ripped apart. As he made his way through the hallway he caught an odor. Or rather, an odor caught him. He could smell his grandparents. Kalman was overcome with nostalgia and a sense of deep melancholy. He could still see the house as it had been. His grandmother was cooking in the kitchen, grandfather Kohane sitting in his old chair sharing stories with the children. Then as suddenly as the scene appeared in his mind – it disappeared – leaving only the darkness and disarray of an abandoned house.

Kalman felt himself not so unlike the house.

He scrambled through the rooms looking for anything he could find. He went into the basement and found some silverware and clothes, grabbed what he could and ran back to his father who was waiting inside the ghetto.

Each night thereafter Kalman's father was able to barter with the peasants for food. The Poles would come around the fence late at night to trade; a silver spoon for a loaf of bread; some eggs and flour for a heavy wool coat; and through it he was able to provide sustenance for his family. Kalman made several excursions to his grandparent's house, and at times he thought he could hear them talking in a room which then fell silent as he entered it.

day of the weeping wind

It had been two weeks since Kalman arrived in the ghetto. It was a warm night and everyone was huddled on the floor of the Rand house. Kalman could not sleep. His stomach ached from hunger and the stuffy heat caused him to sweat on top of the blanket. He felt the walls closing in on him – so cramped that he wanted to scream, to jump up and run out into the night air, to sit in a field under the stars where he could move and breathe freely. He opened his eyes and glanced around the room. His mother and father were at his side. Sarah and Moshe were cuddled in between them. Kalman took a deep breath and exhaled slowly, feeling comfort next to his family. Even in the dirty, cramped conditions, he wanted to be nowhere else. At least in the dark of the night in the tiny box of a house they were left alone. He was with his family, he could feel their bodies next to his, and for that he was grateful.

The next morning Kalman arose before sunrise as he did every day to join the other workers. They met near the old Synagogue where a wagon would be waiting for them. But this morning was different. There was Gestapo everywhere.

"Stand here!" an officer yelled at the group of workers. "Don't move!"

A stream of SS swarmed through the gate and into the ghetto. Shouts and screams echoed through the camp. The soldiers were pulling people from their houses, half asleep and dazed. Kalman glanced around with his eyes and saw a young mother being pulled out of a doorway by two large men. She held a young girl in her arms. The child was terrified and crying hysterically.

"Shut that thing up or she'll be riding the end of my bayonet!" one soldier yelled.

The woman fell to the ground and dropped her little girl. She started to crawl toward her daughter when the soldiers again grabbed her and started dragging her away.

Von C. Petersen

"No! My baby!" the woman screamed. She fought and kicked until another soldier kicked her in the mouth and she fell silent, blood dripping out of her nose and split lips. The little girl sat on the ground, crying out, "Mama! Mama!"

Two older women then picked the little girl up and carried her as other soldiers began herding the stunned people down the street.

"All you men!" The officer shouted at Kalman and the other workers. "You will march to the balcony of the Synagogue and await your orders."

The men stood still for a moment looking at the officer.

"Now! Move!" And guards pushed them through the door which led to the second floor of the Synagogue where the women normally sat during services.

As Kalman stood on the balcony, he could see a line of people filing out of the ghetto. Men, women, children. All carrying what they could of their meager belongings. Their faces were stoic. They seemed in a state of disbelief. Fear and sadness rode their every step.

Then Kalman saw them.

Like specters they appeared before him. Kalman closed his eyes tightly and shook his head from side to side, hoping to shake the image from his sight.

Just a mirage from a hungry stomach.

But when he opened his eyes the scene did not disappear. Not an illusion. Not a mirage. Not a dream nor a nightmare, but reality. Hard, bare, cold reality, flowing unrelentingly from moment to moment as he witnessed a stream of people being led out of the ghetto, hauled into wagons, and carted away. Through the window of the Synagogue, Kalman watched friends and acquaintances, shopkeepers and Rabbi's - people he had known all his life - step into oblivion. And standing within this line of dispossessed souls was his family.

Can not be happening, Kalman told himself over and over, as if by force of will, by choosing not to believe, the procession would stop.

Can not be happening.

But it did not stop.

Kalman stood on the wooden floor of the balcony, his body rigid, his heart racing and his eyes fixed on a sight he hoped and prayed he would never witness. His father, the broad shouldered man who once seemed invincible to Kalman as a child, now stood in line with a sack of pots and pans over his shoulder. A rush of anger and shame pervaded Kalman as he stood with his feet cemented to the ground and his legs paralyzed: anger at his father for allowing this to happen; shame at the sight of this self-made man; a decorated war hero, being led away like a lamb to slaughter – his father! And at the same instant that shame turned to guilt; merciless guilt for sensing even for a brief moment any indemnity towards his *tata*, the man who loved and cared for his family with every ounce of strength he ever had. He could have no more resisted this hoard than a man could drown out the sun by pissing on it. A profound sadness overtook Kalman. His father held Sarah in his arms. His mother was directly behind them and she too had a satchel full of dishes over her shoulder. Moshe was by her side and she was holding his hand tightly.

Kalman began to cry. He wept as he watched his family being loaded into the wagon and taken away. His entire life was in that wagon. His history. His love. His world. Gone. The last time he would ever see them.

The workers continued standing in the balcony until the last of the village had been liquidated. The last person shoved into the cart was a very old, frail man. It was schoolmaster Yoski. The chinless sergeant who had stopped by the gate earlier in the week was shoving him in like a piece of meat, and when the old Yoski slipped and nearly fell off the wagon, the sergeant began kicking him in the backside with his heavy boots while the other soldiers laughed. Kalman closed his eyes. He could watch no more. He could not stand to feel any longer. His heart felt paralyzed. He had entered the realm of limbo, neither wishing to live nor to die, but simply fade away as though he never existed.

As soon as the last wagon had departed, the workers were ushered back downstairs and into the street. They were immediately set to work tearing down the ghetto. For the next several days, the camp was systematically dismantled. Every house, every board, every nail was pulled up and discarded. The entire neighborhood was cleared out like a weed patch. Kalman went about his task robotically. He was alive to be sure; he was breathing, he voided, he felt hungry and thirsty. This was life. But life vacant and numb. Gone was the joy of life. The simple pleasure of lying on the grass under passing clouds, feeling as if you could reach up and grab them. The exhilaration of being next to a pretty girl, hoping to sneak a kiss. These things belonged in a different realm. Even the memory of such things seemed foreign, tainted by the haunting aloneness of these bitter days.

When the last of the bricks had been taken down and every board removed, and the only evidence that the ghetto ever existed was washed away by the worker's sweat, Kalman and the others were remanded to the school gymnasium.

"Sit!" An officer yelled. "Here! Schnell! Schnell! Now! Are you deaf! Move! If you move you'll be shot! Pigs! In rows! Now! Sit in rows! You, here. You next to him. Now! Schnell! Schnell!"

Soldiers grabbed and shoved at the men and boys, pushing them down to the floor. The black pants and jackets the captives wore were dusty and tattered, their white shirts stained yellow with sweat.

One man was grabbed by the beard by an overzealous guard who was enjoying the power of humiliation. "Get down you Hebrew son of bitch! Where's your God now! This is your temple. Now get down and pray!" And he pushed the gaunt Hasid down to his knees. "Join your brothers and don't breathe until I tell you to breathe!"

The bewildered workers were systematically manhandled to the floor until the last one was in place. They knelt on their knees in rows of ten. Ten across and ten to fifteen deep knelt these condemned men; their knees rooted to the earth and their heads extending to the heavens, as flesh and bone bridged between heaven and an earthbound hell..

"Every man empty his pockets. Watches, rings, money. Everything goes out in front of you. Don't think you can hide anything. If as much as a kernel of corn is found in your person you will be severely punished. Do you understand? Now! Schnell! Schnell!"

Each man began emptying his pockets. Kalman sat at the end of the row. As his neighbors emptied their pockets Kalman whispered to them. "Saul, give it to me. I'll keep them for you. They won't check me. I have nothing they want. I'll keep your money until we're out of here."

Rather than giving their money over to the Nazi's, the men around him gave it to Kalman. They knew and trusted him. He would keep it until they got out of the gymnasium. Kalman hurriedly stuffed it in his boots while the SS paraded around the room. In his rush a few coins slipped out of his fingers and dropped to the floor, clinking as they fell. Kalman froze. He dared not look around him, afraid that the soldiers had heard the coins fall to the floor. Nothing stirred. No one heard. An SS guard was making his way down the aisle, collecting the money and goods from the men and placing it in his helmet like a bastard church offering from hell. He was getting closer to the end of the line and to Kalman when Kalman quickly scooped the remaining coins from the floor and stuffed it in his boot. The soldier stood directly in front of him. To the left of Kalman was a man in his 40's wearing what was a rather well fitted shirt and black pants. He was a tailor.

"Empty your pockets," the soldier ordered. "Now take you hat off...and your shoes." The man did what he was told. Nothing was found. The guard then turned his attention to Kalman. He looked at him for a moment. A scrawny boy with not even peach fuzz on his face. He had nothing of worth. The guard passed.

After everyone had emptied their pockets and the goods had been collected, the selection began. "Half of you will stay here," an officer announced calmly. "The other half will be taken to another location." He began walking through the room and with a black pointer started separating the men. "When you are picked you will stand up and go to the back of the room." With the ease of choosing apples off of a tree he proceeded through the gymnasium. "You," he said as the pointer aimed indiscriminately down the rows. "You. And you. You." And so it went. Finally he approached the end of the row where Kalman sat. Kalman tried not to look at him. With the wave of the stick the baby faced officer pointed at the gentleman next to Kalman. "And you," he instructed. "To the back of the room." The tailor stood up, leaving a backpack on the floor. Kalman grabbed it and pulled it to his side as soon as the officer and the tailor were gone.

The remaining men continued half-kneeling on the floor while the others were led out of the back door and loaded into wagons. They were taken to the cemetery and forced to dig a trench with their bare hands. The men knew it was no trench. It was their grave. A cold wind blew across the tombstones and the iron gate squeaked as it swung back and forth. The men started to sing. Softly at first and then growing more and more loudly – they sang. They sang an old Yiddish song, praising the earth and the Lord, and they continued singing until the hole was dug. The SS troops laughed at the men as they sung, but they would not stop. From the gymnasium Kalman and the others could hear the singing. It floated on the wind, deep and harmonious. Then the shooting began. Gunshots. Many, many gunshots. But still the singing continued. As the shots rang out the singing began quieter and quieter, until at last, only one man sang. Then another gunshot rang out and the singing stopped. Even the birds and the stars and the wind wept that night.

The remaining men in the school were then loaded up into wagons and carted off to Tarnow. Kalman had taken the backpack and within it were fine clothes, a coat, socks and a pair of shoes.

When they arrived at the village of Tarnow, a light snow began to fall, covering the ground with a soft blanket of white.

CHAPTER 9

a day of miracles

K alman stepped off the truck, his body chilled from the cold air, and onto the soft white snow covering the streets of the Tarnow ghetto. Looking up he saw a figure approaching from the distance. At first he thought he recognized a familiar face, but his head was cloudy from inhaling exhaust fumes and assumed it was only an apparition. Then he heard his name called out.

"Kalman! Kalman!"

He looked again, trying to focus his eyes. The figure grew closer, until Kalman could make out the outline of a face. A long, thin face. Dark brown eyes. Curly brown hair and a distinctive nose, rather hook shaped with a large hump in the bridge. That nose he would know anywhere, it was Yosel, a friend from Dombrowa.

"Kalman!" Yosel shouted again. "It's Yosel"

Kalman stood, dazed, until Yosel reached him and took him by the arm. "Kalman, you're alive. You're family was so worried."

"My family?" Kalman asked, not comprehending what he had just heard.

"Of course - Your family - Your mother and father - Sarah and Moshe - They're here Kalman - Here in Tarnow - They're all staying at your aunt's old place."

In an instant, shorter than the single flicker of a fly's wing, Kalman's heart sprung alive.

"They're....they're here? Now?"

"Yes Kalman," Yosel told him excitedly. "Here. Now."

Before Kalman could reply, Yosel took him by the arm and led him back to the truck where a large table had been set up by the Jewish Council.

"You must first register, then I will take you to your family."

Kalman went to the table and received his ID card and work permit.

"And where will you stay?" A man sitting at the table asked.

"With my family," Kalman replied with great joy. *"With my family!"*

As he walked to the house with Yosel, Kalman was so excited to reunite with his family that he felt his feet nearly floating across the ground. He could not walk fast enough and his body seemed to be lagging behind. His heart beat loudly like a great symphonic drum but at the rate of a hummingbird. He wanted to run, but was careful not to draw attention to himself, so he lengthened his stride until finally he looked like he was stepping over a great crevasse with each step.

At last they reached the house. Kalman stepped through the door and his mother, brother Moshe and sister Sarah were sitting on an old couch along with a cousin. His mother was so overwhelmed at the sight of her son she was unable to speak. Moshe and Sarah, too, cried with their mother. Filled with such overpowering emotion, Kalman felt himself covered with goose bumps; his skin tingled, even his hair seemed to be tingling, as if his entire body had been charged with a jolt of electricity.

It felt as though his spirit was flowing right out through his skin.

Time stopped.

Inundated with love and joy and relief, the moment rang eternal.

They all waited anxiously for Mr. Willner to get home from the steel mill. When he finally arrived, he had the greatest surprise he could have ever hoped for - his son. With all the family gathered around, Kalman pulled out the rucksack and began emptying the contents onto the floor. Money, jewels, clothes, pieces of silver. His father could not believe what he saw. With the gifts from Kalman they would be able to buy food on the black market and perhaps even secure passage out of the ghetto.

"A joyous day!" his father called out. "A day of *miracles*!"

That night everyone slept soundly in the house which was a mere shack. There was one room with two beds, a couch, a wood stove and a small table. It was wonderful! Only their family lived in it, and though it was cramped, it seemed like a spacious haven.

The following morning, Kalman began work at a local hospital, digging trenches, painting, removing trash, along with various other odd jobs. It was now November of 1942 and winter came with cold winds and heavy snows mixed with rain. Kalman worked every day but Saturday, while his father had Sunday off. Mother and the children stayed in the house, hidden from sight. If you worked you were relatively safe, but anyone who could not work and stayed in the ghetto could be taken away at any time. The Gestapo would show up and round up as many people as possible and ship them off. Off to where no one knew.

There were no stores in the ghetto, which was much larger than the ghetto of Dombrowa. There was nowhere to buy milk or bread. Nowhere to get flour or vegetables. Fruit was but a mere memory. But still they survived. And each day they survived was a miracle. Some of the local Poles dropped food on the ground to help feed the Jews. Many days, as Kalman walked home from work, he often found turnips, beats, cabbage, potatoes, a loaf of bread; perhaps a few eggs or even a small chunk of salt beef. He tied strings around his pant legs so that he could carry more. His father, too, was able to secure food from workers at the mill. Together they scrounged enough to feed the family. At least enough to keep them from starving to death.

As the men and boys worked during the daytime hours, the actions occurring in the ghetto grew ever more frequent and volatile. The Gestapo descended upon the captives without warning; sending some scrambling into tunnels like rats, while others hid in attics, cellars and behind trees. Mothers stuck rags in baby's' mouths to keep them from crying out loud. Old men were dragged out of their beds and shoved underneath like a pair of old shoes in the hopes that the hoard would not find them. But often there was no escape. Young girls were snatched up like rag dolls. The elderly had no chance at all. Being too old and frail to flee, they were easy prey. Women, young and old, rich and poor, the educated and illiterate were drug away, placed in trucks and shipped off, never to be seen again. This was life within Tarnow.

rommelman the lizard

Saturday morning: January 1943

Kalman was sleeping soundly when Mr. Willner burst through the front door. "Kalman, you must get up!" he said with a strained voice. Kalman immediately sensed the tone in his father's voice. A tone that spoke of danger. When Kalman turned and looked into his father's eyes, he understood well the fear that lie behind them.

"Something's happening," Mr. Willner told his oldest son. "Something bad. You must go to work today Kalman."

"But I have no work today Papa."

"Go Kalman. You must go find work today. Take your card and find work, you cannot stay here. I tell you my son, you cannot stay here today."

"And you papa? What will you do?"

"I will be at the mill."

"And mama? And Moshe and Sarah?"

"They will hide. You mustn't worry about them Kalman. They will hide and I will be at the mill working. And you must also be working. You mustn't stay in the ghetto today. You cannot! Now you must get dressed and go. Hurry!"

Kalman dressed and went outside. Standing near the gate was a group of roughly fifty men and boys waiting for work detail. Two young guards stood nearby along with Commandant Rommelman. Rommelman was a greatly feared man. He seemed to be made of cold stone. His features were as smooth and expressionless as carved granite. Light blue eyes peered out behind his thin, needle nose like two pieces of frozen sea water. He had an overbite which made his two front teeth, which were long and yellow, stretch his mouth and thin lips out like that of a dried mummy. He called everyone by "Sir" or "Mama", in a tone of reserved respect, but would shoot them in the back without blinking an eye.

Kalman approached the group and stood at the end of the line just as Rommelman was choosing the men who were to work that day. Rommelman saw Kalman and stepped over to him.

"And who are you sir?" Rommelman inquired with a voice as cold and expressionless as his face.

"Kalman Willner, Commandant sir."

"I see. And what are you doing out here this morning."

"I'm looking for work sir."

"And why aren't you working already? Do you not have a work permit?"

"Yes sir," Kalman assured him as he fumbled in his pockets for his ID." "Here it is."

"If you have a permit, why have you not been assigned a job?"

"I work at the hospital, sir. My commando doesn't work on Saturday."

"Why are you here then?"

"I wish to work, sir. If I work. I eat."

Rommelman looked at him with the cool gaze of a sadistic sociopath. He reveled in his power, the power of life and death, and the life that now hung in the balance was Kalman Willner's.

Kalman tried not to look at him while at the same time not avoid his gaze. Work or leave behind? Live or die? What did it matter to Rommelman? Yet it was Rommelman who was his judge and jury, his savior or executioner, and in a split second the decision whether Kalman would live or die would be made by the Commandant of the Gestapo with less forethought than what he may have for dinner that night.

Rommelman continued to gaze impassively at Kalman with a Reptilian Stare; cold, calculating and utterly void of emotion.

"Good then, Sir," Rommelman finally spoke, his thin lips barely moving as the words slithered out of his mouth. "You will join the others."

"Thank you, sir," Kalman uttered as he quickly joined the others.

"Let them out," Rommelman ordered.

One guard opened the gate while the other led the men out of the ghetto and loaded them onto a truck. A thin, frail looking boy of about seventeen ran up to the gate behind them. Kalman watched out of the back of the truck as the boy spoke to

Rommelman. He was showing the Commandant his papers and Rommelman was saying something to him.   Then Rommelman motioned to let the boy through. The boy stuck his papers in his pocket and started to walk through the gate. He looked up at the truck and caught Kalman's eyes for a moment. Kalman could see that he had a faint smile on his face. Rommelman started to walk behind the boy silently so he wouldn't notice. He was no more than 10 feet from the truck when Rommelman reached into his holster, drew out his Lugar, pointed it directly at the boy with a fully extended arm and steady hand, and shot him through the back of the head. A piece of gray brain tissue and skull fragments splattered onto the bumper of the truck. Rommelman walked up to the body, rolled it over with his foot, and then pounded on the back of the truck with his fist. "Go!"

Kalman could swear the boy still had a smile on his face as he lay on the ground with half of his skull missing. Rommelman could reach him no longer.

an angel and the vacuum of silence

The guard who accompanied the prisoners, a regular Wehrmacht soldier, slammed the door, started the engine and drove off with his stunned passengers. The truck drove out of Tarnow, up a narrow, winding road through a hilly region of bare farmland, and came to a stop overlooking an industrial park. The soldier jumped out of the truck, came around to the back and told his passengers to disembark.

"We are here," the short, stocky corporal announced. He looked to be no older than twenty-two, with short, curly blonde hair peeking out from beneath his helmet, slightly rosy cheeks, and a layer of baby fat slumping out from underneath his tight, black belt. The men and boys piled out of the truck and stood silently while the guard inspected the site. Sitting before them was a line of empty cattle cars, more cattle cars than Kalman had ever seen, stretching down the railroad tracks as far as the eye could see. Kalman knew this was no work site. The guard walked down the tracks for several meters before turning back and returning to the men gathered behind the truck. He stood before them with a great deal of uneasiness, wringing his hands and nervously fumbling with his belt. No one spoke. All eyes were on the young German soldier. He paced back and forth for a few moments and then spoke: "You can't stay here," he mumbled half to himself and half to the others. "I don't like this.....something's not right."

The guard seemed deeply disturbed, to the point that the rouge tint on his cherubic cheeks appeared to have drained to a pasty white. His eyes flashed back and forth from the prisoners standing silently next to the truck, to the cattle cars and back to the prisoners. He rubbed his hands apprehensively over his helmet and paced around in a tight circle. Finally he walked up to the prisoners; "We can't stay here," he informed them again. The men looked at him and did not know what the soldier wanted them to do.

"Come, everyone, in the truck, hurry."

The men did not move. What trick was he playing on them?

"Hurry, he insisted again, half whispering and half shouting.

"You cannot stay here. In the truck. *Schnell!*" We must go!"

Kalman and the others piled back into the truck. The guard jumped in the cab, slammed the door shut, and started the engine, the diesel valves tapping in the cold, still, morning air. They drove up a bumpy, back road a short distance until they were hidden behind a vacant hillside and came to a stop. The guard came around to the back of the truck. "We're here, come, come, you must hurry!" he said as he anxiously scanned the area for any onlookers.

The men jumped out and sitting before them was an empty building – more of a storage shed constructed of whitewashed brick with broken windows. "Everyone come with me," the guard ordered. "Into the building."

Once inside, the men were told to sit against the wall and away from the windows. "We will stay here," the Wehrmacht corporal announced.

A cold wind blew in from the broken windows while the men sat silently against the wall. The building was empty save some broken tables and empty crates. After a couple of hours the guard left the men alone for twenty minutes or so. When he came back he had a satchel of food; soup, bread and some hard cheese.

"This should keep you," he told them.

Kalman was confused and in disbelief. Was this an angel? No matter, food is food, and warm soup with a chunk of meat was a delicacy beyond description. After he finished the soup, he took a couple bites of bread and cheese, and though his stomach begged for more, he wrapped the rest of it in his grandfather's old red handkerchief which Kalman carried everywhere, and placed it securely in the leg of his pants for his family.

Still, the men could not understand why they were there.

And then it began.

Screaming. Women, children, men. Deep barks and vicious growling from German Shepherds. More shouting. Gunshots. The ghetto was being liquidated. Kalman's father was right.

All the men in the building knew what was happening, yet they remained silent. Their families, their friends, all whom they held dear were in that ghetto and they were powerless to help and they suffered in silence. The horrible cries of agony moved from the ghetto to the hillside where the cattle cars sat. Kalman shut his eyes but could not shut his ears. He wanted to crawl out of his skin. He felt himself imploding with anger, fear, and deep anguish, for each anonymous cry, each scream, could be his mother, his baby sister or little brother. Each time a gunshot rang out Kalman felt the heat of the bullet in the pit of his own stomach. The day turned to a dream, a nightmare. *Why was this happening?* He asked himself over and over, but there was no answer. It just was.

As night fell, it began to snow. The sky turned a deep blue and flurries of fire and ice blew in through the broken windows of the vacant building like licks from the devils tongue. The heavy doors of the cattle cars were slammed shut and the train began to move down the tracks. Each turn of the steel wheels brought the people from the Tarnow ghetto closer to hell. As the cattle cars faded in the distance, so did the cries of despair. Soon the hillside fell silent, and the silence was deadening. No one stirred. No one moved. The deep blue sky turned black and the stars began to shine through the thin clouds. Stars had no right to shine that evening.

The cherubic Wehrmacht guard, who was sitting quietly in the corner, stood up and walked over toward the door. "Everyone stay here, I'll be back." He stepped outside. In a few moments he came back and announced, "It's clear, we must go now." All the men stood up and filed out the door and into the truck as the guard hurried them along. "Come, you must hurry before someone sees us!" The men picked up their pace and crawled into the truck. They wanted desperately to get back to Tarnow to check on their friends and family, but equally fearful of what they may find. Once everyone was loaded, the guard started the engine and they made their way back down the short, winding road to Tarnow.

They drove through the gates of the ghetto, which were again guarded by the Jewish Police. The Gestapo was gone. The ghetto was in complete disarray. Doors that had been kicked in were left hanging on their hinges. A scattering of clothing, dresses and coats, along with family pictures in broken frames, *menorahs*, shattered *seder* plates, even a *shofar* which had been run over by a half-track and reduced to dust, were lying on the ground where they had been hastily dropped in the melee. Kalman thought of nothing save returning to his aunt's house. When he finally arrived home, he nervously stepped through the door and into the small living space. The house was as dark and still as an empty tomb.

"Mama," Kalman called out. "Moshe, Sarah." But no answer came back. A vacuum of silence swallowed his voice. The house was empty. They were gone. Kalman was overcome with an unfathomable sense of anguish and aloneness. He collapsed onto the floor and began to cry. The tears burned hot down his cheeks and fell onto the hard floor. He felt as cold as a corpse, as if his spirit had drained from his body. No one was there to wipe away his tears. No one to cradle his head in their lap. Not even the rats would come close to him as he sobbed himself to sleep. They were gone. Never would he see his family again. There would be no reprieve this time. Even in his fitful sleep he cried.

The next morning Kalman was awakened by the sound of the front door being opened. Kalman sat up and through his puffy eyes saw his father standing in the doorway.

"Where is mama?" Mr. Willner asked. "Where is Moshe and Sarah? Where is my family?"

Kalman did not - could not - answer. Mr. Willner ran through the house crying for his children and his wife. "Mama! Moshe! Sarah! Where are you? It is safe now, you can come out," he pleaded. He flipped over the bed and table, as if somehow his family was hiding underneath, and then again ran into the kitchen. "Moshe! Sarah!"

Kalman sat motionless on the floor. Then his father stepped back into the room. His face was as white as snow and his eyes were wide and wild; the pupils dilated into two black saucers. Then he began to pound his head against the wall. He pounded violently until the plaster began to crack and blood spilled out of his nose, eyes, mouth and ears. Kalman sat in horror as this vision of his father pounding his head seared forever into his memory, as the remainder of the day faded into a state of disjointed unreality

deeper into the maelstrom

The following days were but a blur. Kalman listened to people speak, but heard only incoherent words. Sounds without meaning. The solidity of his environment shifted into the sphere of a mirage. Houses, people, even the ground beneath his feet took on the essence of a dream. Time itself ceased to be. The strands which give the illusion of a solid, distinct world; one of individuated parts, separate and distinct, faded as surely as time itself. Kalman sat in bare, raw existence; the proof of his Being made real by the pain of his loss – like the pain of a phantom limb after an amputation – yet accentuated a thousand times over. The light in his father's eyes, who was a mere thirty six years old, had dimmed. The only strand which kept him connected to the world at all was his concern for Kalman.

The two, father and son, continued working; for not to work meant sure death. The ghetto was divided into two camps, A and B. Mr. Willner was remanded to camp A, which was designated by the Gestapo to be for skilled workers. Camp B was for everyone else; the few women and children left, along with those like Kalman, highly dispensable, unskilled labor. The Council placed several occupants into Kalman's aunt's house and he was forced to vacate. With nowhere to lay his head, Kalman wandered the streets for several hours until he finally approached the men of the Council and inquired where he may live. He was told there was a widow with a large house he could stay with. "They have room," he was told, and was sent to speak with the woman.

A short, stocky woman answered the door along with her dog, a fat schnauzer with long claws. The woman had a long hangnail on a purple toe and a large excess of adipose tucked around her round, plump frame. Compared to the others in the ghetto, she looked like a blimp – stick a needle in her and she'd blubber around the room like an untied balloon.

"Yes," she snapped.

"Excuse me ma'am," Kalman began. "I have no place to stay." He paused. "The Council told me you may have extra room." Indeed, she had ample room, for it was only her and her son who lived in one of the largest homes in the ghetto.

"I don't think so," she replied in a short, curse tone. She had somewhat of a simian face, with a protruding upper and lower jaw and long, broad teeth which made the lower half of her face stick out like a chimpanzee's. On top of her head was a patch of frizzy, reddish-grey hair which resembled a hairy mole with a bald patch in the middle of it.

"There is *no* room here," she insisted.

"But..." Kalman began.

"There is no room here!" the woman repeated as she began to shut the door.

Kalman put his foot in the door jam. "I have nowhere to go. The Council told me to come here. I can sleep on the floor. I promise, you won't even know I'm here."

"Go away," the woman snarled. "I have no room here."

Just as she spoke those words, a man walked in a side door. He was a big, strapping young man in his mid-twenties, with broad shoulders and thick, muscular arms. Kalman's skinny frame could have fit under the man's skin twice over. He was wearing the uniform of the Jewish Police. "What's the problem mother?"

"This boy is trying to break into the house. He say's he wants to stay here and won't go away."

Stirred by his mother's words, the big goon ran up to Kalman and shoved him out the doorway. Kalman fell back and landed on the side of his hip. Before Kalman could get up the Policeman leapt on top of him, swinging wildly with his thick fists on Kalman's back and head. After a few minutes of being pummeled by his not-so-gracious hostess' son, Kalman was left bloodied and bruised on the street and the son went back inside.

"And don't come back here you dirty little shit," the woman yelled as she slammed the door shut.

Kalman picked himself up, wiped the blood from his nose, and began to wander the streets in a daze. He was in the midst of a ghetto full of houses but had nowhere to call home. Nowhere to rest his head. After several hours he heard a familiar voice call out.

"Kalman! Kalman, what happened to you?"

He looked up and walking toward him was his old friend Ignet Stieglitz's aunt.

Kalman told her what had happened and she immediately replied; "You come with me. There is room is our place." She took him by the arm and led him to the building where she and her husband and daughter, along with seven young men lived. It was a basement flat with cement floors, no windows and exposed pipes on the ceiling. The seven men along with Kalman slept on the floor in one corner of the room while the Stieglitz's slept on a makeshift mattress made of rags.

Both Kalman and his father continued to work but rarely saw each other. Mr. Willner was at the steel mill and Kalman at the hospital and both lived in separate camps. After Mr. Willner discovered his family was gone that one horrible morning, the light in his eyes faded, and even now the only thing which gave them a spark of life at all was when he ran into his son. That was his one and only reason for going on.

Kalman had been staying roughly two or three weeks in the basement when he and the others awoke one morning to a horrible stench. What they woke up to was a broken pipe and a foot of sewer water. Covering one half of the floor was a standing pool of feces and urine. The men just sat and looked at it. For several minutes no one bothered to even get up, so numb they were to fetid conditions. Finally, Mrs. Stiglietz got everyone moving, and they cleaned the place as well as they could with the rags from the mattress. In less than a week the entire group became violently ill, with high fevers, diarrhea, and extreme fatigue. So sick had they become that the entire household was placed in a makeshift hospital that had been set up by the Council. There was no medicine. No doctors or nurses. Just a room with beds for the sick. So Kalman simply lay on a metal cot, sweating through his clothes, barely able to crawl to the toilet. If the Gestapo had found out and determined that they had contracted cholera or dysentery, everyone would have been killed, and very likely the entire ghetto would have been burnt to the ground. As it was, Kalman and the others simply stayed in the ward until they had the strength to leave, receiving no real treatment whatsoever.

After one week, Kalman pulled himself up and left the "hospital" ward, which was barely a step cleaner than the rank basement he had fled from in the first place. With nowhere else to go and unwilling to return to the underground cesspool, Kalman waited until late one evening and crawled over the fence to Camp A. He managed to find his father's shack, and for the remainder of his stay in Tarnow he slept, hidden under the bed, venturing out only during the day to work at the hospital.

One early morning on the cusp between fall and winter in 1943, a Gestapo guard came up behind Kalman as he was digging a trench, placed shackles on his wrists, and threw him in the back of a truck with a group of others. As they drove out of town, Kalman fought to catch a glimpse of Camp A where his father was staying. Little did he know that when he left the house that morning, it would be the last time he ever saw his father.

He was descending ever deeper into the maelstrom.

CHAPTER 10

the brown cloud

After being handcuffed by the Gestapo while working at
the hospital and accompanied back to the Tarnow
ghetto by the Jewish Police, Kalman was loaded onto the back of
yet another truck with a group of young men and driven out of the
gate and onto an anonymous road. A young man jumped out of the
truck and tried to escape but was gunned down like a rabbit before
he made 10 meters.

> *This is it*, Kalman kept thinking to himself.
> *Finished. So what. At last the misery will end.*
> *I'm done.*
> *Done.*

He glanced back at the ghetto and thought of his father. How he wanted to hold him one last time! To see his smile and hear his voice! But his father was sleeping now, to be sure. Perhaps in his slumber he was in still waters, resting from the painful existence of his waking hours, unaware that his son, the last of his surviving family, was at that moment being taken away from him.

Find peace then, father.

God be with you.

My misery is ending now.

And with that thought, Kalman found his only solace.

The journey in the truck was neither long nor short. It could have been hours or weeks. For Kalman, it did not matter. Night or day, warm or cold, it was all the same, for he sat in limbo, neither fully alive nor dead. There was no going back to what had been, nor moving forward toward new horizons. There was only the unbearable state of the present moment – and like one ravaged by crushing depression, pain or disease – he felt a terrible void. Grandfather Kohane had always said, "Life is lived in the moment." But the moment was the last place Kalman wanted to be. The moment was cursed - life and existence nothing but a sinister joke. His life was not his own. He was an ant ready to be crushed by an elephant's hoof. He sat abandoned and alone.

Soon it will be over.

The end.

And with this, Kalman drifted into a fitful sleep.

Running over a large pothole, the truck bounced violently, throwing Kalman's head, which was dangling in his sleep like a broken chicken's neck, into the side of the truck bed. Jarred awake, Kalman righted his body by placing both hands on the floor of the truck, palms down, wrists bent and elbows locked. The truck hit another hole and Kalman braced himself by stiffening his body and extending his back against the side of the rail. When the ride smoothed out, Kalman was fully awake. It was still daylight, but he had no idea what time it was, or that perhaps it was even a new day. But what did it matter? Time? Hours? Days? Weeks? It was all the same. There was a heavy, sweet smell in the air, not the sweetness of honey or flowers, but a rank, artificial sweetness that burned the eyes and felt heavy in the lungs.

Driving down the road they rolled past an oil refinery. Large cylindrical tanks dotted the site and were connected by a maze of pipes and valves and more pipes, built up from the ground into a skeletal structure of hardened steel. Smoke plumes streamed out of monolithic chimneys and hung in the sky as a brown cloud. When Kalman turned to look down the road past the refinery, he saw the town of Jaslo. As they approached the town, Kalman saw for the first time the makings of a true labor camp. There were mires of barbed-wire fence surrounding the camp, razor sharp and charged with a high voltage electrical current which buzzed through the air like a swarm of angry bees. Guard towers were situated around the periphery of the camp and manned with machine gunners. This was a camp one could not simply walk away from.

The truck passed through the gate and into the encampment. There were people milling about, both prisoners and soldiers, remanding the camp to a bizarre village of the dispossessed. The truck came to a stop in front of a wooden barrack. Guards began yelling at the prisoners; "Get out of the truck you lazy pigs!" The men disembarked and were quickly herded inside. On a small, wooden sign above the door read the word, QUARENTIEN.

Once inside, the men were forced to undress and then systematically inspected like a shipment of fresh livestock. Kalman stood in line behind the others, young men and boys, completely naked, flesh to flesh. Some tried to cover their genitals with their hands to hide their shame, but were only laughed at by the guards. Then the inspection began. Kalman stepped up to a wooden stool, one of many lined up in the room, and sat on the cold seat. With a pair of electric sheep shears, his hair was shaved down to small stubs with a bald track razed down the middle of his head. This was one way the Gestapo used to mark the prisoners. If anyone were to escape, all they had to do is take the cap off to know it was a prisoner.

As his hair fell to floor, Kalman felt more naked than ever.

"Move on! Move on!" the guards yelled.

Kalman rose from the chair and moved down the line. His head was inspected for lice, as well as his armpits and genitals. Then the men were forced to bend over and spread their cheeks so a guard could check for diamonds. With each movement down the line, the humiliation grew deeper. Once this process was complete, the prisoners were herded into a shower where they were doused with a white powder to kill any fleas or lice, and then shoved into a scorching hot steam shower.

After the shower, the men were given prison garb and released into the main camp. Kalman had no more than stepped out the door when a young boy ran up to him. "Kalman! Kalman!" It was a friend from the Tarnow ghetto. He had arrived weeks earlier and worked in the kitchen. Kalman felt slightly relieved knowing someone in the camp, and being that his friend worked in the kitchen, maybe he would be afforded extra food. He began to feel he could survive this place after all, but the feeling was short-lived, for the next day he was shipped out again.

fields of death

Along with roughly five hundred others, Kalman was driven through a hilly landscape with dense forests interspersed with farmland until they reached the small town of Rymanow. Outside of town was a large camp which now sat empty. Rows of barracks, latrines, guard houses and storage sheds stuck out of the ground where potatoes once grew. Only weeds grew now. This would be home for the next five weeks.

"Why do they take us here? To be shot?" A middle-aged man asked Kalman as the trucks came to a stop. "They could shoot us anywhere, why bring us here?" Kalman did not answer. There was no answer. Awaiting them in the camp was a small SS garrison along with Commandant Scheidel, a twisted, sinister man who was never seen without his dog, a monstrous German Shepherd. Within minutes the men were unloaded and lined up before the Commandant, where they were given succinct instructions.

"You are here to work. You will do as you are told. If you do not or if you offer any resistance what-so-ever, you will not leave this camp alive."

With that, the prisoners were remanded to their respective barracks.

On the following morning, after a sleepless night, Kalman found himself engaged in a macabre web of utter insanity. The prisoners awakened before dawn and sent to a large mess hall for hot water and chicory, a bitter, brown brew served in place of coffee, along with a slice of moldy bread. The bitterness of the brew and moldiness of the bread would normally have been entirely inedible if not for the aching hunger which already gnawed on Kalman's stomach, yet it was nothing compared to the foul abhorrence which awaited him and the others as they left the mess hall.

Once outside, the men were led to a field lying on the periphery of camp where Commandant Scheidel awaited them. There was a sickly sweet smell in the air, but it was different than that of the refinery. This odor was more acrid. Organic. And although it did have a faint sweetness to it, it was intensely rancid and stuck heavily to the lungs and skin. Some of the younger boys began to gag softly, while Commandant Scheidel covered his mouth and nose with a silk handkerchief.

After the men were gathered in the field, Commandant Scheidel began to speak, removing the handkerchief only long enough to talk, then covering his mouth again to inhale. As he was speaking, one of the young men began to vomit. Scheidel was incensed at the interruption. Without warning he unleashed his dog and sent it on the sick man. Kalman froze in terror. The dog ran past him and leapt on the man, who was kneeling over and clutching his stomach. Kalman could still feel the dog chewing on his own leg in the snow-covered forest years earlier, and as the attacked man was reeling in agony, Kalman himself grimaced with the pain of empathy.

"Take him away!" Scheidel snarled, pointing at the ravaged young man lying on the ground. Two guards grabbed the boy by the hands and began to drag him away while the dog still gnawed on his foot.

Schneidl began to speak again, informing the workers what their job was to be. The camp had previously been used to house thousands of Russian prisoners, all of whom had since been shot. They were buried in the fields where the men now stood. Now they had to be disposed of. All remnants that the camp and the prisoners had ever existed must be eradicated. The men stood in disbelief. Could Schneidl have said what they thought he said? He wanted them to dig up the bodies and burn them? Surely this could not be. No human being could ask such a thing.

"Are you deaf!?" Schneidl screamed. "Get to work!"

It seemed that this human being could indeed ask such a thing, either that or he was no human being at all, but just another head of the beast. Schneidl was then driven away in a jeep with his handkerchief tightly clasped around his mouth as the men immediately set about their grisly task under heavy guard by the SS, all of whom also had cloths covering their faces.

Several men were given cast iron picks with wooden handles. The others were left with nothing other than their hands as tools. No gloves, just flesh, bone, muscle and tendon to dig out the corpses. Among the men were cobblers who had used their hands to fashion leather into fine shoes; a surgeon and a tailor who had honed the fine motor skills of their digits into a high art; piano players and violinists whose highly tuned hands once filled the air with beautiful music; as well as stone masons, carpenters, and blacksmiths who helped build civilizations. There were young Yeshiva students whose virgin hands knew nothing but pen and paper, along with bakers and butchers who utilized their skills to produce fine meals.

These hands, these highly evolved extensions of the human mind, hands which had stroked lovers and carried children, were reduced to this ghoulish task that not even the lowest life forms were ever forced to perform, not alone forced by their own species to perform. Only humankind could claim heir to such brutality.

Humankind. Only humankind, capable of such great achievements, could also be capable of such great evil.

But Kalman was not pondering such things. He was in a state of chronic shock, with only the primitive, unconscious will to survive fueling his existence. To ponder such things, to wonder why, meant sure madness. Some things are incomprehensible, even to those experiencing it.

The morning sun was peaking over the low-lying clouds, illuminating them like a patch of iridescent mushrooms, and as the warm rays hit the ground, evaporating the moisture from the soil, the fields began to exhale a fine mist into the air. A surgeon, a rather rotund man, a man accustomed to giving orders, not receiving them, had informed his fellow prisoners while in the truck, that no reasonable man – not even the Gestapo – would ask of him manual labor. His skills could be applied just as easily to a German than a Pole or a Jew.

"Surely they have special plans for me," he assured his compatriots. And as the other men gathered their picks and were about to set out into the fields, the surgeon, blinded from danger by his own impenetrable ego, raised his concerns to the guards.

"I believe there has been a mistake," he began. "I must speak to the Commandant. I am a surgeon - trained in Vienna. I can offer my services to your men, those who have been injured in this great war."

A young lieutenant, impeccably groomed in his black uniform, velvet cap and knee-high leather boots, approached the doctor and stood directly in front of him. After looking him up and down for a few moments, the officer stepped even closer to the surgeon until their noses were nearly touching.

"I see," the lieutenant said. "And what services are these? Do you want to cut into German flesh? Is that what you are asking?"

"No...well yes...not exactly..." the surgeon mumbled.

"Please doctor, say no more," the officer replied, gesturing the doctor to be silent by raising his index finger to his lips. "Perhaps you could watch over the others," the officer announced.

"Yes. Yes. I can do that. Yes. I have had many, many people working under me. They could do nothing without me," he continued, trying still to convince the officer of his importance.

"Very good then," the lieutenant answered. At that he stepped back to talk quietly with his men. In less than a minute, two guards came over to the doctor and grabbed him by the arms.

"What...what is this?" he stuttered.

"You will watch over the men," the officer laughed.

They then drug the surgeon to a large tree and wrapped a thick rope around his neck. The man struggled and shouted, "No! No! This cannot be. This is a mistake! A mistake!" He continued to yell as they hoisted the rope over a heavy limb and began to pull the doctor off the ground. The rope pulled tightly around his neck and the screams turned to a low gurgle. Kalman watched as the man's face turned red, his eyes wild and bulging, and finally turning to a sickly bluish color as the doctor fell silent.

The officer turned to the other prisoners. "There he will be better able to watch over you. Anyone who would like to offer their services may join him."

~

In the ensuing weeks, over 150 prisoners were either shot or hanged. The prominent surgeon's nightmare ended on the limb of an old tree. Hardly the Tree of Life Kalman had heard about as a boy, and as the crows picked at the dangling corpse overhead, Kalman's nightmare was only beginning.

The fields themselves seemed to be crawling as the decomposing bodies began to seep into the ground. Rats and packs of wild dogs competed for the spoils. The fresher bodies were often swollen like ghostly balloons, exploding when a pick hit them, emitting a horribly foul gas into the air. Others were stiff and unmovable and had to be dismembered, while many others began to congeal into a yellowish gel beneath a swarm of writhing maggots.

Kalman picked and dug and finally was given the task of pulling gold out of the mouths of corpses with a pair of pliers. Sometimes as he spread the mouth open the entire jaw would tear off the face. He was no longer on Earth, but in Hell. Only the faint hope that he would survive and escape the hell kept him alive at all.

The stench became so bad that farms for miles around had to be abandoned. For over three weeks Kalman never bathed, never took his clothes or wooden shoes off, until at last he began to resemble a corpse himself. When the last of the bodies had been exhumed and burned in giant bonfires, their ashes were spread over the fields as fertilizer. The surviving prisoners then went about demolishing the camp, brick by brick, plank by plank, until the entire camp was dismantled. Even the pipes underground had to go. Peasants were allowed to take whatever they wanted, as long as it was taken away.

Once the barracks were taken down, the prisoners were left to sleep outside on the ground and were given only enough food to prevent starvation. Commandant Schneidl was conspicuously absent from the fields, but once the corpses were removed and the work in the camp had begun, he was back with his vicious dog, taunting the prisoners, many of whom who were mauled for nothing more than Schneidl's amusement, and left to die from massive infections.

the bath and the butterfly

One night as Kalman lie on the damp earth, huddled in the fetal position to retain his body heat, a tiny caterpillar crossed his path. His first instinct was to crush it. Perhaps even to eat it. But as he watched the furry creature scurry along the ground, its sticky feet grasping and pulling the body forward, Kalman could not find it within himself to do either. Instead he simply watched it pass.

He reached up and stroked the fine fur with his finger and the caterpillar curled up into a tight ball, not unlike the position Kalman was in, and remained perfectly still. It had nowhere to hide. It had no defense. Kalman sat transfixed on this tight ball of fuzz. At that moment, only Kalman and the wooly-worm existed. Slowly the caterpillar uncoiled itself and began to crawl away. Kalman hoped it would survive its trek across the barren ground and find haven in a thicket of leaves where it could become a butterfly.

On the next morning came a big surprise. The men were to bathe in the river. The guards lined the haggard prisoners in a single row and made them run to the creek. Once there, the men disrobed and jumped in. After the initial shock of being immersed in frigid water, Kalman felt relief from the cold currents as they washed away weeks of dirt and grime and decay.

And then it began.

Rocks. Rocks began to fly through the air and into the river. Several of the men were struck in the head, one of whom who had been knocked unconscious and began to float down the river until other prisoners grabbed him. The stones came from the guards. They were playing a child's game with human beings as targets. The only way to escape the flying rocks was to keep your head underwater. But as soon as you came up to breathe, you were like a bobbing target. Ducks in a pond. Fish in a barrel. The guards laughed and laughed at their little game, and for the remainder of their stay at Rymanow, the prisoners were the unwitting ducks and fish.

After five, horrendously long weeks, the work at Rymanow was complete. Every bare scrap of material had been removed. Every nail, brick, board and body was disposed of, leaving the camp looking like nothing other than empty farm land ready to be seeded. The physical evidence had been erased. The memories could not be. The field of decay would turn green again. The earth would reclaim itself and all the scars of empty graves would disappear. Yet what was lost there could never be reclaimed, not for the living or the dead, and even after the earth itself is swallowed by the sun, there will still be a cold spot where the Fields of Death once stood.

Near extreme physical and emotional exhaustion, the remaining prisoners were finally rounded up one morning and shipped back to Jaslo. Out of the 500 men and boys who started, less than half survived. Upon leaving Rymanow, Kalman felt like he was being sent from hell back to paradise.

paradise

Immediately upon arriving back in Jaslo, Kalman was sent back to quarantine where his head was shaved once again. Louse eggs were hatching in his scalp and the Ukrainian guards laughed as they took photographs for their scrapbook. After delousing and showering under hot steam, Kalman was released into the main camp. Although still a labor camp, Jaslo was pristine compared to the brutal and primitive conditions at Rymanow. Jaslo was more like a large town surrounded by barbed wire and armed guards. Kalman milled about the streets for a short while when his old friend from the cafeteria happened upon him again. Finding a friend in difficult times is not unlike finding water in an alkali flat, a landscape normally so devoid of moisture that white alkaline powder leaches up from the earth and covers the ground with its filmy residue, making even a desert seem like an oasis. To be greeted with a smile is a great gift. It can help retrieve your spirit from hell, and such was the case with Kalman upon his return to Jaslo.

That evening at the soup line when the guards weren't looking, Kalman's friend slipped him an extra piece of meat, and as much as the smile did for Kalman's spirit, the food did for his body. After dinner, Kalman filed into the *appelplatz* to be counted along with the others and then sent to their respective barracks. The hard, wooden bunk and wool blanket were a step above the muddy ground at Rymanow, and Kalman slept soundly through the night. At 4:00 AM the barracks were awakened by the *kapo,* a fellow Jewish prisoner who was put in charge of the barrack on the merit of his own sadistic nature. Cruelty was usually the one, defining trait of *kapos.*

"*Aufstehen!*" he yelled, rousing the haggard men from their beds.

A light soup and chicory was served in the mess hall and everyone was back at the *appelplatz* for morning count by 5:15 sharp. Sometimes they would stand for hours in formation before the Commandant would meander over to count them. After being accounted for, Kalman was marched to the main gate with a large group of other men and loaded onto a truck which drove them over a short mountainous pass to the refinery. Here they were met by the commandant of the refinery along with his Ukrainian guards. Kalman was immediately introduced to the officer's strange ways. Before beginning work, the prisoners were subject to the bizarre ritual of getting on and off of the truck as quickly as humanly possible.

"Auf! Hinunter! Zuruck!"

"Up! Down! Back!" The Commandant roared. Anyone struggling to get back on the truck or faltering as he stepped down was beaten by the guards with wooden batons, who stood by anxiously like hyenas at a fresh kill. Five times they would get off and on the truck. Ten times. Twenty times. The men hopped up and down out of the truck bed to the ground and back again like trained monkeys as many times as necessary to satisfy the Commandant's twisted brain. Kalman was still young and fast, and could hop in and out in a spit second. Anyone too old or too weak to perform would be beaten. If it happened again, they were taken away, never to be seen again.

To be quick.

To work hard.

This meant you may be allowed to live another day.

Another rule which was strictly enforced, but explained only in retrospect, was that anyone caught with a shiny object; a knife, a spoon, a tin cup, anything at all, would be shot on the spot. Usually the only property a prisoner was allowed to have was a tin spoon and mess tin to eat with. After several men were shot after such an object was found on their persons, the others were told that such an infraction was punishable by death. Kalman had learned long ago that anything could be punishable by death. Such were the Gestapo games, and one cannot negotiate with absolute power. In this case, the Germans did not want anything shiny which could be seen from a bomber flying overhead, never mind that the entire refinery was a huge amalgamation of twisted metal.

papa

The men set out to work. A railroad track was being built from the main line to the refinery, and Kalman's job was to dig a trench along the line. Armed with picks and shovels, the men worked in pairs, one with a pick and one with the shovel, switching occasionally to lessen the fatigue. For several months, through scorching heat, cool breezes, wind storms, hail, rain, and always with the sweet stench of refined petroleum hanging in the air, Kalman dug through the dirt like a mole, sun up to sun down, returning to Jaslo each evening for a meager meal and the *appelplatz* head count. There were cold showers available and a latrine which consisted of a trench stretching down the middle of a barrack with a wooden plank running down the center of it to sit on. There were 300 to 400 prisoners in each barrack with bunks three high and two across and a single blanket for each person.

The camp was split into two sections, one for men and one for women, separated by a barbed-wire fence and gun towers. For an hour or so each week they were allowed to mingle with each other; husbands met with their wives, fathers spoke with their daughters, while Kalman came upon a distant cousin who had also grown up in Dombrowa. For an hour each week the two would walk through the camp and reminisce about life before the occupation; of Sabbath spent with family; of listening to grandfather Kohane's stories and savoring grandmother's hearty meals. For a few moments each week they could almost remember....remember that they did have a life once -that it wasn't a dream - that is was real.

Love and laughter; family and God.

It had existed once.

In another place.

Another time.

Another world.

One day as the two were talking, lost in shared memories, they wandered beyond the perimeter of the guarded area. Their memories were quickly interrupted by loud shouting and the sound of a machine-gun being cocked into position. A few more steps and they both would have met their end. Luckily the gunner wasn't too trigger-happy and they were allowed to step back to the safe zone unharmed. On another day with a different gunner the outcome could have easily been much different. Life was cheap. On a whim, a life could be extinguished without so much as the blink of an eye.

As time went on the Commandant began to tighten his grip on the camp. He told everyone, "I am your father," and demanded to be called *papa*. No longer were the men and women allowed to get together, but he did let them talk a few minutes through the barbed-wire fence. Any minor infractions were dealt with by the whip. Everyday people were dragged in the middle of the *appelplatz*; women, men, young and old; forced to pull their pants down and receive 40 or 50 lashes from "papa" while everyone else was made to circle around them and watch. Beatings and hangings were commonplace, and rations were reduced to watery soup with perhaps a tiny chunk of potato or turnip. Again, hunger became Kalman's constant companion, and thoughts of food were unceasing.

One early morning on a drizzly day, the entire camp was harshly awakened by the guards who kicked and screamed their way through the barracks. Everyone was forced to gather in the *appelplatz* where papa was awaiting them. The Commandant's mechanic, a Jew, had stolen papa's car in the middle of the night and escaped.

"Your father has treated you well," the Commandant told the audience of captives. "And this is how you reward me?"

Everyone was standing in the typical rows of five when papa began picking people out of the group to be escorted to the center of the square. Kalman stood in the fifth row when papa pointed at him. He began to step forward when papa yelled, "No, not you! Him! The man behind you!" Kalman stepped back as the other man stepped forward. After there were roughly twenty people herded into the square and forced to kneel down, machine guns opened fire on the group, shredding them like skinny balloons filled with red paint.

"Today it is twenty." Papa informed the survivors. "If anyone tries to escape again it will be a hundred and after that a thousand."

The prisoners were then dispersed back to their barracks while the murdered bodies were scooped up and disposed of. Kalman had seen so many dead bodies that he began to see the look of death even in the living. Had the Commandant not changed his mind and Kalman not stepped back into the row of five, he too would now be a punctured balloon. Soon afterward the camp learned of a group of roughly 2000 people who were gunned down outside of Tarnow. Among them was Mrs. Goldman. One by one, everyone from Kalman's past was being exterminated. His past itself was being exterminated.

He thought briefly of the Goldman sisters.

Had they survived?

Who could know?

The thin line between life and death itself was rapidly disappearing.

CHAPTER 11

cattle

Near the end of November, 1943, as Kalman approached his eighteenth birthday, the entire camp at Jaslo was assembled in the *appelplatz*. The body count was taken, but once completed, the prisoners were not released as usual. There was no morning meal, however paltry, no time to relieve themselves or return to the barracks to ready for the day. Instead, they stood. Minutes turned to hours and still they stood. Kalman's back ached, his feet hurt and his legs began to cramp. Those who were too old or too weak to stand were either beaten or simply succumbed to death, crumpling softly to the ground from where they stood.

As evening approached, the cold, dry air began to spit large, wet, snowflakes onto the weary prisoners. As the snow fell onto Kalman's head and melted down his face, he tried to capture the droplets with his tongue to quench his thirst. He began to wonder if they would be forced to stand in the square forever, stand until their bodies gave way and fell limply to the ground. Time slowed to a torturous trickle.

Then it began. Guards rushed into the *appelplatz* and ordered the prisoners to form a line. Like cattle they were herded through the gates and out of the camp. Every 10 meters stood two armed soldiers on either side of the line to ensure no one escaped. For two kilometers they plodded their way through the snow, not knowing where they were going or why. Once they rounded a hilltop, a line of closed cattle cars came into view as far as the eye could see. Still no one noticed, but as the head of line approached the cars and Kalman saw that they were being forced into the rails, he knew what was happening. The railcars had swallowed his mother, brother and sister in Tarnow, had swallowed them and taken them away, and now they were going to swallow him.

Each car was less than 29 feet long, made of solid strips of wood roughly the size of 4X4's. A large, sliding door with a heavy locking bolt adorned the front entrance while the back wall had a tiny, grated vent near the ceiling. There were no windows, save a tiny rectangular opening which was barely large enough for one person to peer out of. Kalman was loaded onto a "round-roof" car which looked like an oversized bread box with fixed steps attached to the front entrance. One out of every ten or twelve cars were round-roofed, while the others had flat tops with no steps, making it difficult for small children and the elderly to load on to. Those who weren't helped on by others were beaten savagely by the SS.

One by one they were herded onto the cars, upwards from 80 to 100 people in each car. Children began to cry, "Mama, I don't want to go in here. Where are they taking us?" But all their mothers could do was silence the children so as not to draw the wrath of the Gestapo. Kalman stepped into the cold, bare, car and stood near the back wall. More and more people filed in, squeezing their way past others, jockeying for space where there was none, until finally the entire car was packed with people, standing shoulder to shoulder, front to back, and face to face. So closely packed they stood that one could feel and smell the hot breath of others on one's face. There was no room to turn, nowhere to hide, nowhere to walk. Finally the heavy door was slammed shut and the deadbolt locked down.

Within minutes, panic set in. Old men and women began wailing, "God in heaven! God in heaven!" Children wept while others, feeling the walls close in tighter and tighter, tried to get away, to push through the crowd, yelling and screaming, "I must get out! I can't breathe! Please let me out!" But there was nowhere to go. They were trapped within a coffin on steel wheels. Cut off from the world, shock began to set in and the railcar grew silent except for a low moan of anguish. They stood in the darkness of the car for hours, each moment stretching into an eternity, until at last the cast iron hitch engaged with a loud clang and the car suddenly jerked forward. The train slowly gained speed as it click-clacked across the metal tracks, while inside the cars the walls grew ever more constrained.

Day turned to night and back to day again. The train traveled steadily in an unknown direction, frequently coming to a stop and sitting idly for hours on end before starting up again. People began collapsing from exhaustion onto the cramped floor which was already strewn with the bodies of those who had expired. Still there was no room to sit or lie, and Kalman's legs began to feel like solid wood. People were defecating and urinating and the stench became malignant, eating away at what little air was left in the car. Kalman felt like he was being slowly asphyxiated, drowning in the bottom of an overflowing outhouse. By the second day, the dead began to outnumber the living, and the surviving captives began to pile the corpses in the corner, and that pile in turn became the latrine.

For three days and three nights the train traveled until finally it came to a stop.

Final destination: Auschwitz.

arrival in hell

Kalman and the others were lying on the filthy floor, half dead and half alive, when they heard the heavily bolted lock unlatch from the outside. The door to the railcar swung open and a rush of cold air filled the compartment, partially reviving the lethargic passengers.

"Steigen Sie aus! Steigen Sie aus!"

"Get out! Get out!" The SS troopers yelled.

"Schnell! Schnell!"

"Fast! Fast!"

The bewildered prisoners struggled to their feet while the soldiers backed away from the stench emanating from the enclosed compartment. Kalman felt himself rise like a piece of crumpled newspaper slowly unraveling under its own volition, void any of conscious control what-so-ever. He stumbled down the steps onto the platform and the butt of a rifle met his jaw followed by a sharp thud on the top of his head as a baton struck down on his skull, nearly knocking him to the ground. He staggered away, his head pounding, dazed and disoriented. All was utter chaos. Standing in a mass of other prisoners, flood lights blazing down with blinding fury, SS troopers shouting, kicking, dragging and beating prisoners, German Shepherds ripping at people indiscriminately, Kalman neither knew where he was or who he was. After 72 hours in the death train and now bombarded with such mass insanity, his mind was at once crazed and benumbed.

People of all ages were gathered on the platform, old men and women with tattered clothes, young women dressed in their finest clothes and families with young children. Those departing from Kalman's transport were all pale and sickly, their clothing soiled and ragged. Those who had arrived on earlier trains and had shorter journeys were relatively clean, but everyone, each man, woman and child, bore the same look of utter despair and horror.

Everyone was shuffled into a long line. Kalman felt something warm and sticky trickling down his face and onto his shoulder. Standing next to him was a young father with soft, green eyes. He was holding his little girl who looked to be no older than two years old. She was dressed in a yellow dress and a knee length jacket, with shiny black shoes with brass buckles and a purple ribbon in her bright, red hair. She had a button nose and rosebud lips which were quivering with fright. Her soft, smooth skin was highlighted by rouge cheeks and she had her little arms wrapped tightly around her father's neck. In one hand she clutched a small stuffed animal, a green turtle, her prized possession. Every night for two years her father had tucked her into bed with "Mr. Turtle." The turtle and her father were the only things she had left in this world.

"Everything in the box!" An SS trooper bellowed. "All your belongings must go in the box!" He instructed the prisoners. Boxes were placed along the line and everyone began dumping their pockets, watches, jewelry, even hair pins into the box. The little girl held tightly onto her turtle until a *kapo* yanked it from her hands and ripped it open with a knife.

"Any jewels in here?" He sneered.

The little girl did not even cry. She had no cries left in her.

The father's eyes became wild with rage as the trooper dropped the disemboweled turtle and walked away. Then, as if a soft veil fell over him, the father's eyes became glassy and his face was imbued with a sense of calm. He held his little girl tightly against his chest, her soft cheek nuzzled into his, their hot tears mixing as one salty stream. Then the father stepped out of the line and began to slowly walk away.

"Halt!" A rabid *kapo* yelled out. "Halt!"

But the father kept walking, slowly and steadily away from the line. The *kapo* ran up and slammed the butt of his rifle into the father's back, but still he kept walking. An SS officer who was watching the scene unfold stepped up behind them, pulled out his revolver and emptied three cartridges into the father's back which exited out through the daughter's chest. They fell to the ground, silent and still. Their suffering was over. They were at peace now and nothing could ever come between them again. The father's love for his little girl had been stronger than death itself.

The others in line weren't as lucky as they moved steadily towards an impeccably dressed Gestapo officer with round, wire spectacles. Kalman could see the officer motioning with his fingers as the prisoners approached him; left, right, left, right, right, his thumb and finger jerking indiscriminately. Those he directed to the right formed a separate line and those to the left yet another. Children, the elderly and most of the women went to the right, for what reason, they did not know. More able-bodied men and certain women went to the left. Children were being pulled from their mothers, wives from their husbands, brothers from sisters; screaming, begging and crying not to be separated. They knew, deep within they knew, it would be the last they would ever see of their loved ones, yet they were utterly powerless to help them.

Finally Kalman approached the head of the line and stood before the officer.

"Wie alt?" The officer asked. "How old?"

"Eighteen."

"Welche Arbeit?"

"What work?"

"Laborer."

The officer looked at him for a moment, and then motioned to the left with his manicured hand. Once chosen, Kalman joined the group to the left, his mind still stunned from the lights, noise, hunger, thirst and pain. Then they were forced to run. Kalman could barely walk after being cramped in the train for so long, but as the guards began shouting and beating the crowd, his legs began to piston up and down like an automaton's. They ran and ran through the frigid cold, snow blistering their feet, flood lights blazing down on them, guards and dogs barking violently. Razor sharp fence lined each side of them, and behind the fences were rows upon rows of rectangular, brick barracks. In the distance, five round chimneys stretched into the sky, bellowing an acrid, brownish smoke into the air. Kalman could feel the warm, sticky blood dripping onto his shoulders and back from his head wound. He did not care any longer. To live or die meant nothing. He wanted only for the suffering to end.

161273

The prisoners were finally herded into a large, brick building. This was Quarantine. The building was empty except for a cold, concrete floor and a single light bulb hanging from the ceiling. Once inside, the doors were locked and the prisoners were left alone without food, water or blankets. Kalman collapsed onto the floor, and though he was beyond exhaustion, he was unable to sleep. He curled into a tight ball to fight the cold, tossed and turned and drifted in and out of an anxious slumber. His jaw ached terribly and the blood from his head congealed into a sticky mass. There was nothing to do but lie on the concrete floor and wait.

Before dawn, the barracks were awakened by four SS troopers. Each prisoner was given a piece of stale bread and a cup of tepid chicory, and then instructed to go outside. Two chairs had been set up in front of the building and sitting on them were SS men who had small electrical devices in their hand. A line was formed in front of them, and though Kalman could not see what was happening, he heard a strange buzzing noise like that of a dentist's drill. When he approached the SS in the chair, he was instructed to hold out his left arm. The guard grabbed Kalman's wrist with one hand, and with the other, which was holding the electrical device, began tattooing a number into Kalman's forearm. It felt like a bee sting as the ink was injected into his skin, and in less than two minutes, it was over. When he was finished, Kalman was shuffled into the back of a transport truck with the others. He looked down at his arm. In a sickly bluish color, the shade of deoxygenated blood, the numbers **161273** stared back at him. He rubbed it with his fingers and could feel little bumps forming from the needle and ink. In the eyes of the Nazi machine, he was no longer Kalman Willner. He was **161273**.

herring

Once everyone was stamped and loaded onto the truck, they approached a brick guardhouse sitting ominously under a wide expanse of sky dotted with high, cumulus clouds. The mid-section of the guardhouse was comprised of the main tower, a one story, square structure with a four-sided pyramidal roof. A glass observation deck sat beneath the roof and underneath the deck was a solid brick foundation with two windows in the front. An arched entranceway sat at the bottom and expanding on either side of the tower were two long corridors approximately 50 meters long with v-shaped roofs. From Kalman's vantage point the guardhouse looked like a ravenous monster poisoning the sky above it, the two windows appearing as eyes gazing out beneath a pointy head and the archway a bottomless, gaping mouth, while the two side structures became the legs of a spider.

As the truck passed through the archway and into the mouth of the beast, Kalman felt himself being swallowed. This was Birkenau - Auschwitz II - a massive complex with row upon row of long, rectangular brick and wooden barracks divided into still more sub-camps by lines of high voltage barbed wire fence. They drove past a warehouse where prisoners were loading what looked like huge bales of human hair into trucks until finally coming to a stop in front of one of the nondescript barracks. They were quickly unloaded and marched into the building where they were forced to undress. Once again Kalman was shaved of his hair, including his genital area, checked for contraband, deloused, showered under steaming hot water and given a striped shirt and pants, wooden shoes, a flimsy jacket and a round cap. His body had been violated so much he no longer knew where his body ended and the Gestapo horror began. The boundaries were vanishing, just as the boundary between earth and hell had been torn open by the Führer, the Austrian crapehanger. Kalman's essence of a human being was being drowned out by the Nazi killing machine, where cruelty to others was a virtue.

That evening, the group was placed in Block 14 along with other prisoners, a wooden structure bereft of any comfort and dead of spirit. Lining each wall were long rows of three-tiered bunks made of narrow, wooden planks. Even the wood looked diseased. There was no running water and Kalman was going mad with thirst. There was a brick fire pit in the front of the building which had some cold, charred twigs in it. Even if it had been fully ablaze it was barely large enough to heat a dog house. Rats scurried across the floor and no one seemed even to notice. Nor did the rats pay notice to the humans. In this desolate hell, the rats and the humans were on equal terms.

As night fell, the *kapo* ordered everyone into the bunks. Kalman crawled into a top bunk along with fifteen other men. They were squeezed together like herring, with no room to move, stretch, or barely even to yawn, and were forced to lie on their sides just so they wouldn't be stacked on top of each other. The man at the head of the bed was elected as the caller. Every half hour or so he would call out, "turn," and all fifteen men would turn to the other side in unison. All night long they turned back and forth like a grotesque cabaret. Kalman could feel bed bugs bite into his skin but was too cramped to even reach down and scratch. After a few hours of fitful sleep, when it was time to turn again, the man next to Kalman did not move. Kalman shook him for a moment but he did not respond. He was in a sleep from which there was no return, so Kalman juggled to roll the body over so he would not be staring into the face of a dead man. By the following morning two more had died and their bodies were shoved out of the bunk and onto the floor.

The prisoners were awakened by the *kapo* and herded outdoors to be counted. Those who had died during the night were taken to the crematorium where their flesh would be incinerated into ashes. Kalman stood next to a slightly older man from Hungary who was gazing up at the chimneys bellowing their continual flow of smoke.

"We come by train," he mumbled to himself and to Kalman. "We come by train but we leave only through the chimneys."

cloth and stones

After the living and the dead were accounted for, the men set out to work. From sunrise to sundown they carried heavy stones from one end of the camp quarter to the other, roughly 150 meters, back and forth, carrying a rock to one end, laying it down, picking up another rock and carrying it back. Only the blisters forming on their hands from the rough stone and on their feet from the wooden shoes were more painful than the mindless futility of their task. They would stop at midday and were allowed a small ration of watery soup and stale water before starting up again on the endless chain of stones.

"Why do they have us carry stones if they don't use them for anything?" Kalman asked his Hungarian compatriot.

"We are mules. They weed out the weak and the sick. If you can carry stones then you can work. If you can't then you go to the ovens. You can't see them from here, but there are five crematoriums working all day and all night. Where do you think the women and children have gone? The old men and the sick? They never even made it to a barracks. The ovens must be working at all times. If a train does not show up then they go through the camp for new victims. The gold they pull from the teeth. Even the hair from the women is shaved and sent to be made into cloth."

"Into cloth?" Kalman murmured, remembering the huge bales of hair he had seen in the warehouse.

"Cloth. They use our wives', mothers' and daughters' hair to make cloth. They are not human, these Gestapo pigs. Himmler was here not long ago. He is the demon in charge. Even hell would not have him."

Day after day Kalman carried stones from one end of the corridor to the other and back again. Guard dogs ensured that no one languished behind; those who did found their flesh and bone ripe picking for the fangs of mans' best friend. Kalman instinctively stayed in the middle of the procession and away from the frothing mouths of dogs. Thirst crawled through his body like a voracious raptor, creeping slowly at first, and then seizing him with extreme anxiety. His very cells were screaming for hydration.

Bathroom breaks were given in shifts once or twice a day. The latrine was housed in a single barrack with three long, wooden planks extending from one end of the building to the other. There were two rows of holes in each plank which emptied out into a trough. As there was no plumbing, the trough was emptied out by the prisoners with buckets, and Kalman could barely remember the bathroom at the Polish school he had refused to use as a child because of the filth. There was nothing of privacy in the camp, and even the most private of acts were designed to be humiliating. Yet they adapted. Kalman felt like an animal. Less than an animal. Where he went to the bathroom meant nothing.

Each day the prisoners would arise to the same routine, the counting of the dead and the living, watery soup and chicory, followed by endless hours of carrying stones back and forth, over and over and over under the vengeful eyes of the Gestapo and their slobbering dogs. As Kalman struggled with the heavy rock, day in and day out, he would fall into a trance. The only hope was to survive one more day. Survive until liberation. But what liberation? He wondered. Was the world aware? Did they care? And what of the world? His world was already gone; it had vanished as surely as a puff of blue smoke in a gust of wind. There were no other worlds.

For five weeks Kalman labored within the Quarantine Camp, carrying stones from sunup to sundown, and returning each night to the vile barracks. Each time he stepped through the front door he was met with a slogan painted across the roof beam; *In bloch mutzen ab* - **Hats off in the block**; followed by, *Sauberkeit ist Gesudnheit* - **Cleanliness is health**, scrolled across the next rafter, and the severely twisted motto, **Be honest** - *Sei ehrlich*, after that.

Even in the latrine such banal slogans were to be found, such as, *Verhalte sich ruhig*, **No noise**, painted on the back wall behind a row of fetid toilets.

"What? We may shit too loud!" The old Hungarian laughed. Even Kalman laughed for a moment, and for a brief instant the laughter made him feel alive.

Behind the Quarantine Camp lay the remainder of Birkenau, a series of *lagers*, or sub-camps, which opened onto a central road called the *Lagerstrasse*, each separated from one another by electrical fences. Here sat the women's camp, a Gypsy camp, a medical camp where an unimaginable fiend by the name of Doctor Josef Mengele, the Nazi Angel of Death, along with other murderous physicians, carried out horrific experiments on human guinea pigs, including women, children and twins. There was a family camp, a death camp, the crematoriums, all the makings of hell on earth, and though Kalman could only see the top of a few buildings beyond the confines of his own corner of this hell, he knew what must lie beyond. He knew but could not comprehend. It was unbelievable even to those who were in it.

Each night Kalman would squeeze into his bunk with anywhere from nine to twelve other men and felt so cramped he could barely breathe. And each night three or four men would die in their sleep. In Auschwitz, there was a very thin line between sleep and death, between the living and the dead, and the only thing which differentiated one from the other was the painful awareness of existence those who still drew a breath must endure. Each day saw the arrival on new prisoners to Block 14; the young and the old, the weak and the strong, the religious and the secular, the educated and the unlearned; and each one bore the same vanquished look in their eyes. The gaze of the lost ones. Armageddon had arrived but there was no Messiah. If a new shipment of humans was delayed on any particular day, perhaps by an interruption in the rails, a selection would take place within the camp to replace them. The ovens could never grow cold.

The process was always the same. The SS would come into the barracks and everyone was told to undress. One by one the prisoners would file across an officer or camp doctor and anyone whose butt bones were sticking out was ordered into the corner and taken away. On five separate occasions Kalman was selected to join the condemned men, but rather than going into the corner as ordered he would quietly meander back to the main group. Never was he stopped by a guard. This itself was a miracle.

At the end of the fifth week, Kalman was selected again, but not for the ovens this time. He still had some work left in him, so he was rounded up with a group of others and shipped to Auschwitz III – Buna, the labor camp. It seems that the meat on his bones had saved his life in this bizarre, twisted world which he had been thrust into. Miracles come in many forms.

Chapter 12

bread and a movie

Change is inevitable. Life in flux. That is the norm. The seasons change. The leaves change. People come into our lives and step out again. Sometimes they reappear and sometimes they do not. New life is born unto the world and passes away as surely as the sun rises each new dawn. The only constant is the passage of life to death, that is assured, and the journey from the crib to the grave is but a brief moment in the shadow of time - an illusion within the eternal.

The tighter we hold on, the more illusive our lives become. Our hopes and dreams, fears and anxieties, melt like snowflakes under the hot sun. Yet it is precisely these hopes and dreams and fears which breathe life into the eternal and animate our miraculous existence. We may always ask why, though we are uncertain even of the questions, and the circle of life sometimes smiles upon us, just as surely as it can rain down daggers.

In Auschwitz, there was very little difference between life and death, and miracles were hidden and illusory. The only thing which distinguished life from death was that to be alive, to exist, meant to suffer. That was proof of one's existence. But to survive one more day brought the faint hope that freedom would return; that at some point in time the madness would end. Life itself would not die as long as hope remained, however miniscule that hope may have been. But hope itself can cause pain, especially when that hope is extinguished.

Near Kalman's last days at Birkenau, a fresh shipment of prisoners arrived. Among them was a young Polish man, not much older than Kalman. As Kalman sipped on his watery soup one morning, the man sat next to him and started to talk. He was from a small village outside of Krakow, a Yeshiva student from a devout Orthodox family. "My family is dead," he began. "My mother, my father, my brothers and sisters, they are all gone. My God is dead. He has forsaken us. What is it that I should live?"

Kalman said nothing. There was nothing to say.

The next day the SS guards entered the barrack to make a selection for the gas chambers. The young Yeshiva student was selected. As he walked out the door with the other condemned men, Kalman caught a glimpse of his eyes. There was nothing in them. No shimmer. No energy. No hope. He was heading to the crematorium, but he was already dead. After the damned men had been escorted out of the barracks, another selection was made. Kalman was one of the chosen.

The prisoners were taken outside and placed onto trucks. Kalman kept thinking, "This is it, the end." And in a way, he hoped it would be. By the end of 1943, he just wanted it to be over. If anyone would have come to him, an SS soldier or a guard, and said, "I'll give you as much bread as you want to eat, just bread with water, and I'll let you sleep as long as you want to sleep, and then I'll let you watch a movie, and after that I'll shoot you." Kalman wouldn't have hesitated for a second. Life was no longer a miracle. The only miracle was surviving another day, and if given a choice, it was a miracle most would have gladly given up for bread, sleep and a movie.

buna: kapos and fear

After a short drive, the truck carrying Kalman and the other prisoners approached Buna-Auschwitz, a large camp built to house slave laborers for the I.G. Farben synthetic works factory, a massive industrial complex a few kilometers from Birkenau. The chemical conglomerate had built an oil and rubber factory near Auschwitz so they could capitalize on the labor. The SS was given three Reich marks a day for unskilled prisoners and four Reich marks for skilled men. The company also provided basic food and provisions to keep the prisoners alive.

Kalman was stunned to see a Jewish orchestra playing as they drove through the main gate into Buna. *What madness is this?* He wondered, not knowing if he should cry or laugh. It was like watching goldfish swimming in battery acid. Congenial songbirds in vacuum of darkness. It did not seem possible. But then, the impossible, the unbelievable, was *status quo* in the twisted, barbaric world of the Third Reich.

The men were unloaded and lined up in the *appelplatz* where they were sorted and assigned to their respective barracks. Kalman was remanded to Block 34. He was equally as stunned to find the relative cleanliness and comfort of the camp as compared to Birkenau. Block 34 was a brick barrack roughly the same size as those in Birkenau, but instead of 2000 people stuffed inside, there was only a mere 220. The floors and walls were spotless. Bunks built three high and two across lined each wall and were separated by a middle aisle. Each man was assigned a separate bunk and given a straw pillow and wool blanket.

The *kapo* of Block 34 was an acerbic German Jew by the name of Alfred Mädel. Due to his German background and mastery of the language, he was designated barracks leader by the SS. In Buna, as in the rest of the camps, the bottom feeders of society were often placed in semi-official positions of power. They were the liaisons between the common prisoners and the Gestapo and were given better food, quarters, and sometimes even access to camp brothels which were stocked with female prisoners. The *lagerkapo*, or chief *kapo* of the camp, was a German criminal. A handsome devil, debonair and learned. Also a rapist and a murderer. That he raped and killed women before the war was of no concern to the SS, but that he had suspected Communist ties was, and for that reason he was placed in the camp. That he could rape and murder was a bonus for the Gestapo. Here was a man they could trust.

As with all the *oberkapos*, or overseers, he helped maintain order, often with his feet, fists or a club. Fuelled by envy or rage, ignorance or perverse pride, the *kapos* were often cruel and sadistic.

A failed student in prewar times now had license to beat teachers. A poor man could now maim the rich. A homely man could crush the face of good-looking one. A man who had education, wealth and looks but who looked down on everyone he felt inferior to now wielded the power to annihilate. Poets and writers were made to eat paper rather than food, and artists were burned for their visions. This was humanity turned upside-down. Creativity was subversive to the State. It may prompt people to think - to question - and that would not be tolerated by the State, and was therefore crushed beneath the Gestapo Anvil.

And distilled within each and every one of them, *kapos* and *häftlings* alike, was great fear. The *kapos* afraid of losing favor with the SS, and the *häftlings* - the rank prisoners - the dispossessed ones; devoid of home, family, country and identity; fear of everything *except* death. For it was not death they were afraid of, but greater suffering. They lived with constant, gnawing anxiety that at any moment sheer terror would envelop them. The terror that comes with complete vulnerability; an open wound in an acidic world. Fear of merciless beatings, starvation and torture. Fear was the great controller.

mädel and the face of a ghost

Alfred Mädel stepped into Block 34 to address his men. Roughly 5'8'' tall with a hook nose and beady little eyes, he wasted no time. "You are here as workers for the Führer. That is the only reason you are alive. Never forget that. You will be given your assignments tomorrow. You will do what you are told when you are told to do it. Any resistance, laziness, theft, or anything I don't think is right will be severely punished. Do I make myself clear?"

That night Kalman slept soundly in his new bunk. At 4:00 in the morning Herr Mädel whisked through the barrack, pounding on the bunks with his club.

"*Aufstehen*! Up! Get up now!" He screamed.

Kalman was on the top bunk, so was the first to rise. While standing on the second bunk he made his bed with military precision, the blanket squared and cornered with perfectly sharp ninety degree angles; the pillow flattened to a specific height and width and measured with a wooden stick. He hopped down and the man in the second bunk began making his bed. Kalman dressed and ran outside to shine his shoes with tar that was kept in a large bucket. The shoes themselves were made of hard leather with wooden soles. The men had no socks but were given rags to wrap around their feet. After finishing his shoes he went to the food line where he was given a piece of bread with blood-sausage and a cup of chicory. The food was better than in Birkenau. The gnawing hunger never ceased, but unlike Birkenau, the food at Buna was sufficient to sustain the body enough so that it could work. One of the benefits of corporate sponsored slavery.

As Kalman hungrily swallowed his last piece of *blutwürst*, he looked up and saw the face of a ghost. Or so he thought. Nearly choking on his sausage, Kalman forcefully swallowed the dry, greasy horsemeat and rubbed his eyes with his fists. He looked up again and realized that the face was now staring back at him. But it was no ghost. It was an old friend from Dombrowa! Dombrowa, the village of his youth. The home of his heart! The world which he had nearly forgotten. And now it all came back to him within the soft, kind face of Ben Fishman.

Ben was two years older than Kalman. He came from a very religious family and had a special sense about him. He always seemed connected in a way others weren't. Connected somehow to a power greater than himself. He never preached nor boasted of his piousness; an extremely intelligent boy who could converse with a learned Rabbi concerning the scriptures and felt equally comfortable talking with the most simpleminded peasant about the changing of seasons; a young man of great humility who walked with quiet spirituality.

This is how Kalman remembered him and he was almost afraid to see him now, see what the world had done to him. Ben had always been tall and thin, but now he looked like nothing more than a bag of skin. But as Ben walked up to his old friend, Kalman saw the brightness of his eyes had not dulled. Here within Ben Fishman, the spirit still dwelled, even if now it was covered only with a bag of skin and a striped uniform.

"Ben?" Kalman inquired, still not believing his eyes. "Ben, is that really you? I thought you were a ghost."

"Skinny as a ghost I suppose," Ben laughed lightly. "But I'm afraid no more ghost than you my friend."

My friend. It had been so long since anyone had called Kalman *friend*, he'd almost forgotten what it was.

"Don't run away," Ben quipped. "I'll be right back. Can't have dirty shoes you know. I have an appointment with a bucket of tar."

After tarring his shoes and getting his bread, Ben joined Kalman for a few moments before morning count began.

"Here Karl," Ben said as he handed Kalman a small piece of his own bread. "You look like you could use this. They feed us better here. Have to keep the workhorses working you know."

For an instant Kalman felt himself back in Dombrowa, sitting in the Market Square on Sunday eating fresh bread from the bakery. The moment was broken when Mädel stepped outside.

"Watch that one," Ben warned. "He can be fair or he can beat you to death. Just do what you're told and stay clear."

coal, rags and whips

By 5:00 AM the prisoners were standing in the *appelplatz* for morning count. The SS officers and guards were on hand along with the *kapos* to inspect the men. The *häftlings* stood in formation while each barrack leader sounded off.

"Forty-five *häftlings*, two dead, one sick," Mädel shouted with his head held high, as the well-dressed officer approached the group from Block 34. Each barrack *kapo* repeated this drill until every man had been accounted for, after which the prisoners were assembled into their own respective work units. Kalman was assigned to a group charged with unloading coal from railcars. Each company was then marched out in strict formation past the camp orchestra.

"Hats off!" Each leader yelled to his men as they approached the main gate to be counted once more by the SS. Once through the gate the caps went back on and the men relaxed to a normal walk as they made their way two kilometers to the factories.

The brittle snow crunched beneath Kalman's shoes and the wooden soles offered no traction, causing him to nearly slip and fall while traversing a small hill. Ben grabbed him just in time, saving Kalman both from falling and from the beating which surely would have followed. As Kalman regained his balance, he looked up just as the industrial park came into view. There were five tall smokestacks spewing burnt coal in front of a large, brick, chemical plant. To the right of that were two huge storage bins that looked like massive upside-down thimbles. Railroad tracks cut through the complex and there were various sheds, buildings, warehouses and oil tanks dispersed throughout the park. The frozen ground was covered in a thin layer of dry snow which had turned gray from the sooty air.

A cold, steady wind blew through the camp, shifting the snow-covered ground like icy sand dunes. The prisoners marched through the main entrance and into the I.G. Farben complex and quickly shuffled over to a long line of coal cars. Supplied with wooden shovels they set about unloading the black chunks of compressed dinosaurs and prehistoric swamps out of the bellies of the open cars.

"Kalman," Ben told his friend. "When you get in, dig yourself a space in the corner of the car where you can stand up, then start digging the coal out, it'll be easier. Think of it like a piece of cheese, start at the corner and eat your way down, it's easier on the back and it'll go much quicker. Show 'em how much you can work."

Kalman understood perfectly what Ben was trying to tell him. Work hard. Show them what you can do, but don't get too close. That's the best way to stay alive.

Ben helped hoist Kalman onto the car and handed him his shovel. Kalman started digging in the corner, pounding the tip of the shovel into the coal with the heel of his foot and sweeping it up and over his shoulder onto the ground. It was not so unlike the loads of manure he had spread for the farmer. Once he dug down to the bottom of the coal car, he was able to get a better angle with the shovel and the work progressed quickly. By mid-afternoon, the wind had picked up, and each time Kalman swung the shovel overhead, a layer of coal dust flew off the blade and onto his face and body. Before long he was covered with a thin layer of coal dust, and the whites of his eyes peered out beneath the blackness of his face, while his hands grew clumsy and weak from the bitter cold.

By late afternoon the muscles in his back were twisted in a knot and burned with fatigue. The afternoon soup made no more of a dent in the constant, howling hunger in his stomach than would a single peanut fed to a starving elephant. When the day's work was complete, twelve hours after they had begun, the *häftlings* were rounded up and marched out of the industrial maze and back to Buna. Kalman's feet had grown numb from the cold and he could barely feel his toes. After being counted twice more by the SS, and each man had been accounted for, those who had made it back and those who had been beaten or hung, they were fed another portion of watery soup and remanded to the latrine to clean up.

By the time Kalman returned to Block 34, his feet had begun to swell and when he took the rigid clogs off, the flimsy rags wrapped around his feet had stuck to newly formed blisters the size of grapes. By the third day of this, the rags themselves were frayed to bare thread and Kalman's minced feet stung with every step. That evening Kalman spotted four strips of cloth lying on a windowsill. Making sure that no one was watching, he quickly grabbed them and hid them under his blanket. In the morning he wrapped one of the rags on each foot and stuffed the other two under his pillow.

Had he stuck with the two rags on his feet, Kalman would have been safe, but Mädel noticed the rags missing. After a quick search of the barracks, he found the two remaining strips of cloth under Kalman's straw pillow. Mädel went into a rage. While Kalman was out digging coal, Mädel's fury grew stronger, and by the time the prisoners had returned to Buna, he was a full-blown madman.

As soon as prisoners were released from their work units, Mädel turned his malevolent gaze onto Kalman. When the final evening count was finished and Kalman was back in Block 34, Mädel violently grabbed him by the arm and pulled him to his bunk. Kalman was taken completely off guard. Mädel yanked the pillow off of the bed and exposed the two strips of cloth which he had replaced earlier in the day.

"What's this?!" he yelled vehemently, the purple blood vessels under his pasty face ready to burst.

Kalman's heart raced. Adrenaline pumped through his body. He wanted to run, to hide, but there was nowhere to go. He felt like a mouse cornered by a rabid cat.

His fellow prisoners looked on as Mädel dragged Kalman down the aisle into his private quarters. Once inside, Mädel stripped Kalman's pants down and threw him across the desk. Kalman froze onto the hard, wooden desktop as Mädel reached into his closet and grabbed a *Peitsche*, a thin leather whip. With one swooping motion, Mädel's arm swung from high overhead, down and across his body, landing the whip onto Kalman's buttocks. The hard, leather strap beat down on Kalman's fragile skin with a piercing crack and the sting of fire. Never had Kalman felt so alone and exposed. The leather whip kept beating down on him. By the third crack the skin began to tear off of his butt, sticking to the leather strap and spreading Kalman's blood onto the wall and Mädel's face. Like a wild dog, the smell of blood fueled Mädel's brutal fury, and he continued to beat down on the boy. After the seventh swing, the pain and shock became too much, and Kalman's mind mercifully gave way and he passed out. Mädel continued to whip him until Kalman's buttocks were nothing but exposed muscle, like a freshly butchered loin steak. When he was finished, Mädel drug Kalman out of his quarters and dropped his slumped body onto the hard floor.

"*Ruhe im Block* - Quiet in the Barrack!" Mädel yelled before returning to his quarters and slamming the door shut.

love of a friend

After the lights were dimmed in Mädel's room, Ben Fishman quietly crawled out of his bunk and tip-toed to where Kalman lie unconscious. Ben slipped his elbows under Kalman's armpits and carefully dragged him to his bunk. He hoisted him onto the second bunk, and then crawled onto the one above him. After a couple hours passed, Kalman slowly gained consciousness. His backside stung horribly and he felt something rubbing on it. He turned over and sitting next to him was his friend, Ben, who was gently cleaning the wound with his own saliva. Kalman moaned and slowly lay his head back down on the pillow while Ben continued cleaning the wound.

"It's alright Karl, you're going to be OK," were the last words Kalman heard before drifting back into a stupor.

4:00 AM. Mädel was pounding through the aisles, banging on the bunks with his stick. *"Aufstehen!* Everybody up! Get up!" He yelled before returning to his quarters. Ben quickly arose and made his bed, then helped Kalman off his bunk. "Come, Karl, you must get up now." Kalman resisted for a moment, disoriented from his ordeal the night before. "Here Kalman, I'll help you. You must get up."

Though he could barely move, Kalman understood what his friend was telling him. He must get up. To be sick in Buna meant to exit through the chimneys in Birkenau. With Ben's help, Kalman struggled to his feet and got dressed while Ben made his bed for him.

With Ben supporting him by his side, Kalman slowly made his way out of the barracks to tar his shoes and eat before heading to the *appelplatz*. Every step he took sent knives piercing into his buttocks, but still he kept moving. He managed to make it through the day, and for the rest of the week, Ben tended to Kalman's wounds with great care. If not for the love of his friend, Kalman would surely have died from infection.

Mädel acted as if nothing ever happened, but simply sneered as Kalman limped passed him. Mädel the Master, cherishing the power *die Peitsch* wielded in his scrawny little paws.

After enduring a week of constant pain, Kalman's wounds slowly began to heal. Sunday rolled around, the *häftlings* only day off, and the men were ordered into the barracks for inspection and selection. Everyone was stripped naked and filed passed an SS officer and a camp "doctor." Anyone with more bone than meat, anyone who was ill, was told to go into a separate line.

When Kalman walked up to the physician; the young, well-dressed doctor looked briefly at his face, and then turned his attention to Kalman's red and scarred backside.

"*Recht*," the doctor announced. "Right."

The right side was the *musselman* line, the express to the gas chambers. Kalman started walking to the right, then as the doctor was busy inspecting the next prisoner, he hurriedly turned direction and walked back to the bunks. He held his breath, waiting for the officer to shout, "Halt!" but miraculously nothing was said. He was safe...for now.

saved by bricks

The following morning after being counted in the *appelplatz*, another SS officer went through *zu fünf*, the standard columns of five men, and picked out one hundred of them to become brick layers. Kalman was one of the chosen. He was remanded to work group, or *Commando* 109, where he met the group leader, a short, bald German with loose jowls hanging from his formerly fat face. Kalman knew he was a criminal by the green inverted triangle sewn on his shirt sleeve. Whereas Jews wore the yellow Star of David, criminals wore the green triangle. Communists and other political prisoners wore a red triangle; Roma, vagrants and other non-conformists wore black; homosexuals pink and Jehovah's Witnesses purple. Everything within the camps was organized with the precision of an ant colony.

The work leader counted his men and ordered them to form two lines, after which they were marched in strict military formation passed the officer at the gate.

"Hat's off!" the short German criminal yelled as they passed the gate.

"Thirty-three prisoners in *Commando 109*," he informed the officer.

As they walked to Buna, the frigid wind picked up and sliced through Kalman's thin jacket, chilling him to the bone. A bitter, Arctic blast bore down on southern Poland and each day prisoners were freezing to death. Kalman, weakened by hunger, fatigue and the wound on his backside, felt he may be next. But as fate, luck or chance would have it, he was spared the icy fate of many others. As apprentice brick layers, the men of *commando 109* were assigned to a workhouse where they were taught the basic skills of masonry. For three weeks they laid bricks with artificial mortar, huddled within the heated building as snow and ice beat against the windows. Kalman was also moved from Block 34 and out of Mädel's murderous reach and into Block 10, which had been set aside for the brick layers. Shielded from the cold and from Mädel's *peitsch,* Kalman's wounds healed and he slowly regained a bit of strength.

Each night as Kalman lie in his bunk, he would listen to the humming of the electric fence outside. Two or three times each night the humming would be interrupted by an indubitable pop - the loud, transient buzz of a human body being jolted by the hot wires. For many, the anguish simply became too great, and after the floodlights were dimmed, they would sneak out and run toward the fence. Once they passed into no-mans land between the first set of barbed wire and the electric fence, the magnetic force of the high-voltage wires would ensnare them - pulling them into the wires like a giant, electric bug zapper. Kalman envied them at times, knowing that their suffering was over, that they were finally out of Auschwitz, but he could not find it within himself to jump into the wires. To live or die meant little, but he would not die by his own hands.

Chapter 13

thunderous geese

K alman would not take his life by his own hands, not by electrical fence or otherwise, and indeed it was his hands which kept him away from the crematoriums and *Durch den Kamin,* out through the chimneys. As long as his hands kept busy laying brick, he was of some use to the Reich. The wounds on his butt healed but the mark it left on him never entirely would. At times his jaw, which had met the butt of a gun his first night in Birkenau, still ached so badly he could barely chew his food or sleep at night.

Kalman was assigned as an assistant bricklayer to a small group of Italian masons; two middle-aged men with children of their own and the other slightly older than Kalman. The two older masons always wore a day old beard and smoked incessantly. They bickered back and forth all day long in a Northern Italian dialect and Kalman had no idea what they were arguing about. They acted like a couple who had been married a few years too long. They were forbidden to talk to Kalman, but still managed to treat him like a human being.

For the remainder of the winter Kalman's job was to keep the stove stoked with wood and coal to keep the mortar from freezing, and this in itself was a blessing, for each time Kalman tended to the fire he was able to warm his hands and feet. Miracles were indeed hidden, but they did exist, even if in the form a brick fire. And each day one survived was a miracle in itself. He helped slab the mortar and stack the brick and slowly winter turned to spring. On occasion the Italians, at the risk of their own lives, would slip Kalman a boiled egg or a piece of bread with horse meat; and these small morsels of food were worth more to him than all the gold in the world.

By the time summer rolled around, Kalman felt as if he had lived his whole life in Auschwitz, or rather that Auschwitz had consumed what life he had. Nights of the new moon opened up the sky to a brilliant display of flashing stars, but even these began to resemble the dim flicker of flood lights, and the cool breeze of new dawns was tainted by the acrid odor of burnt flesh. He had all but forgotten what a blade of green grass or the blossom of a flower looked like, for nothing of this sort could survive the barren world of Buna-Auschwitz.

In August of 1944, flocks of a new bird began to visit the sky over the I.G. Farben complex; birds constructed of metal which announced their arrival by the mechanical whir of propellers. Kalman was busy laying brick when a camp alarm went off. The civilian workers, along with the three Italians and all of the German guards and SS ran to cement bunkers to take cover, while Kalman and the other *häftlings* were left out in the open with no place to hide. A swarm of Allied bombers, over one hundred B-17's flying in formation like migratory geese edged their way toward Buna. Kalman nearly shouted with joy when he saw the planes approaching. The war had finally come to them. They were no longer alone. The impenetrable walls of Auschwitz and the Third Reich had been broken. Perhaps freedom could be won. *They were not alone.*

When the slow-moving bombers were directly overhead, they began dropping a barrage of five hundred pound bombs onto the complex. Kalman crouched behind a half-finished wall when the unmistakable shrill of falling armament whistled through the air. Then the explosions began. One after the other the shells landed on the ground with deafening fury, nearly knocking Kalman onto his back. He jumped up and began running while the thunderous blasts ignited all around him. In a state of sheer panic, Kalman quickly ran into a tool shed. Feeling he was soon to be blown to smithereens, he grabbed the first item he saw, a wooden bucket, and placed it over his head as he ducked beneath a work table. The bucket had been full of water and Kalman was drenched from head to toe, then another series of explosions went off right outside the shed. The vacuum created by the blast sucked all the air out of the building, as well as all of the water off of Kalman's body. In an instant he was dry. Then the bombing stopped. The only thing left was the ringing in his ears. That and the holes in the ground and the buildings left to rubble after the nearly 670,000 pounds of bombs dropped on Buna that day.

Kalman stumbled out of the shed while the guards were still in their bunkers. The initial jubilance he felt was replaced with shell-shock, and he looked skittishly up to the sky like a rabbit whose cage was just plummeted with firecrackers.

After the 'all clear' alarm sounded, the SS crawled out of their holes and quickly rounded up the *häftlings*. Every prisoner, alive or dead, had to be accounted for. Kalman was put to work clearing rubble from the shattered buildings. His hands were shaking so badly he could scarcely hold his bowl of afternoon soup. That night he barely slept, and when the electric fence popped, claiming another victim, Kalman nearly jumped out of his bunk.

snip

The following day Kalman did not lay bricks as usual, but was sent for perfunctory training in the art of defusing bombs. It seems that not all of the 500 pound explosives had actually exploded, and now they needed to be defused and carted away. This job was left to the *häftlings*. Kalman's brief introduction to the task hardly made him an expert, but this was of no concern to the SS.

"One way or the other the bombs will be defused," Kalman overheard one guard tell another. "Either with a snip-snip or a kaboom they'll be out of our way."

"If these monkeys hadn't already been paid for by Farben," his compatriot laughed, "we could get rid of a bomb *and* a pig at the same time."

Once the training was completed, Kalman was led out to one of the active shells.

"Go for it," the guard told him as he handed Kalman a pair of pliers. "It's all yours."

Kalman began digging around the shell so he could get to the casing on top. Once he had cleared away enough dirt, he carefully unscrewed the nose casing to expose the firing mechanism inside. His hands were still shaking from the day before, and now they seemed to be jumping around with a mind of their own. He looked at the confluence of wires and tried to remember which one he was supposed to cut, assuming the instructor had even told him the correct one to begin with. He fumbled through the wires with his ten, jumping thumbs, separated the wires, then took the pliers with one hand while holding the hot-wire in the other. He tightened his grip, held his breath, then shut his eyes and pulled.

Snip.

All clear. The bomb was defused and Kalman still had his body parts. He had to remind himself to breathe again before struggling to his feet and out of the hole. One of the guards was cursing because he had lost the bet: Kalman was still standing.

All in a day's work.

~

a number and a noose

After all the bombs had been carted away and the rubble cleared, Kalman went back to work with the brick masons. Day in and day out for twelve to fourteen hours a day, stopping only fifteen minutes at noon for soup. By the time his body hit the bunk at night, his mind was already sleeping. Each Sunday a new selection was made for the gas chambers, and each time Kalman barely escaped with his life. Whenever a new guard was assigned to *Commando 109*, Kalman kept a steady but averted eye on his overseer, making sure to work extra hard. If they saw you could work and do what you're told, there was a better chance of being left alone. Even if you made a mistake they may overlook it. But if you got on their bad side, the guards or *kapos* would beat you to death for breathing wrong.

Kalman's jaw ached so badly he felt like someone had stuffed it with hot lead. He dare not tell anyone, for any sign of weakness would bring on the human predators, and it seemed some of them had developed an unholy sense of detecting weakness and for picking up the scent of fear. It was as though many of the *kapos* and SS fed on fear and misery, gaining strength from other's despair. Power was psychotically intoxicating to some, while still other guards secretly drank all day just to drown out the suffering around them. Trouble was, you were never sure which was which or who was who until it was too late.

A month passed and the bombing was all but forgotten, when one morning in mid September, the hum of warplanes again filled the skies over Buna. A swarm of B-24 Liberators edged their way towards the IG Farben plant as alarms began sounding on ground.

The SS scrambled into their bunkers, while the *häftlings* were left out in the open to fend for themselves. The sky opened up and began raining lead. When the bombs reached the ground, the earth shook with deafening explosions, sending plumes of smoke and dirt high into the sky. Terrified, the *häftlings* began running, seeking cover wherever they could find it. One of the main gates had been left open in haste. Kalman and a group of other prisoners quickly ran out of the plant complex, into the open fields, and lay in a ditch.

After the attack, the prisoners stayed in the field for awhile, afraid of further bombings. When everything seemed clear, they slowly made their way back to the plant, but were stopped by SS troopers before they reached the gate.

With rifles drawn, the SS ran up to the prisoners.

"Halt! What are doing out here? It is forbidden to leave the plant."

"They were trying to escape," a scrawny Gestapo guard announced.

"Is that so?" An officer remarked. "Come here, all of you," he ordered.

One by one the officer wrote down the *häftlings* numbers which were tattooed across their arms. "We'll deal with you later," he told them before escorting them back to work.

That evening while assembled in the *appelplatz*, the numbers taken down by the officer where read off by the camp commandant. Kalman's number, however, was not called. The officer had miswritten it by *one number*. After the numbers were read, each man was ordered to the middle of the square.

"These men were caught attempting to escape. Do you know what happens to prisoners who try to escape?"

The men stood terrified.

"They are hung."

A noose was then placed over each man's neck and they were strung up like animals and left hanging for a week. Everyday when returning from work, there were always two or three corpses hanging in Buna for all the prisoners to see. But each time Kalman passed these condemned souls, he knew he could have been up there with them. One number. Only one, single number had spared him from the fate of the others. It was too much for Kalman to even comprehend. A miracle of chance.

guilty

Summer passed and the cool days of autumn arrived. Sporadic aerial attacks on Buna continued and Kalman sniffed out and defused many unexploded bombs along with his usual work as a bricklayer. Hunger and thirst were his constant companions. He still had meat on his bones, but each day his body consumed more of itself to stay alive and keep working. In October of 1944, word got to the barracks that a group of prisoners assigned to one of the crematoriums in Birkenau had revolted. They were all killed by the SS, but not before destroying the crematorium and a few Gestapo with smuggled explosives first. And just like the first bombing raids, the rebellion had brought some sense of hope to the *häftlings*.

Block 10 had become a depository of the lost and forgotten. Men came and went on a daily basis. Some ran to their deaths on the hot wires. Others were hung for some minor infraction or beaten to death by a crazed *kapo*. Many others were selected for the gas chambers of Birkenau and a few remained on as slave laborers like Kalman. Some prisoners even held a *din torah* and put God on trial. They found him guilty.

Winter came early and brought heavy snows and frigid winds. On one particularly cold Sunday morning, the *häftlings* gathered in the barrack for selection and were inspected for lice, as was normal procedure. One older prisoner had louse eggs on his head and genital area. All of the prisoners were ordered to grab their blankets, pillows and clothes, and to take them outside. While the naked men stood in the blistering cold, their clothes and blankets and pillows were burned. Then they were herded to cold showers followed by delousing with caustic powder. Kalman was shivering so badly that his jaw began to ache horribly. He had expended so much energy trying to stay warm he could barely stand up. The entire barrack was quarantined and deloused while the men again stood outside. Prisoners began turning from red to white and finally to blue. Some died from exposure and others lost toes from frostbite. Kalman switched from one foot to the other and wiggled his feet to keep the blood circulating, and finally, when he was nearly ready to give up, they were let back into the barracks. He slept so deeply that night, that for a few short hours, he did not exist at all.

Near the end of 1944, the Red Army was quickly approaching Auschwitz, and Himmler ordered the camp liquidated. Any prisoners which had not been executed and burned, alive or dead, were ordered into the *appelplatz*. A heavy snow fell onto the gathered *häftlings* as they were marched out of Buna. With nothing but the meager clothes on their backs, the prisoners made their way to an unknown destination. For most, it would be the last walk they would ever take.

CHAPTER 14

march of death

January 7, 1945

Snow fell onto the *appelplatz*, blanketing the hard ground with a layer of white powder and melting into a film of icy perspiration as it struck the beleaguered *häftlings*. The snowflakes did not appear as frozen angels, appearing from the heavens in soft, geometric purity; but rather as crystalline devils which bit the skin with their frigid edges. The invisible, formless wind howled and carried within it the weight of mountains; a cold, furious weight which bore down on the sick and exhausted prisoners as they stood in formation like limp statues.

By the time movement began, the *häftlings* resembled stick figures clad in toilet paper, yet these stick figures were brothers and sisters; daughters, sons, fathers, mothers and lovers. Nameless, faceless and seemingly forgotten.

"Who will die by fire or ice?" the scriptures had asked during the high holy days.

Now it had come to pass. The Gestapo had already disassembled the ovens in a hasty attempt to hide their atrocities and the acrid stench of burning flesh had dissipated. The fires had been extinguished. Now the elements themselves conspired against the prisoners as they marched out of Auschwitz and into the countryside. The dim, gray sky opened into a heavy wall of snow and the light flurries became a raging blizzard. In a virtual whiteout, the *häftlings* trudged through three to five foot snowdrifts, barely able to see their hands in front of their faces.

The outline of SS guards straddling either side of the prisoners appeared as shadowy ghouls through the blinding snow; wrapped in heavy trench coats and duck-billed winter caps; their faces hidden behind scarves and goggles. Intermittent flashes of blue and orange fire pierced through the whiteness as gunpowder exploded out from the bore of rifles. Anyone who fell behind, stumbled on a drift, or staggered outside the line was immediately shot, and a trail of bodies began dotting the landscape as the prisoners continued on their March of Death.

Throughout the day and into the night they plodded on. The snow began to wane, but the ferocious wind continued to howl. Kalman could hear the muffled voices of his fellow prisoners, some gasping for breath, others imploring God to relieve their suffering while still others cursing that same God.

"Come papa," he heard one man plead with his father. "We must continue. You mustn't stop." For several hours the man continued to beg his ailing father to keep walking, until at last the son himself grew too weary to speak. When the old man finally succumbed to fatigue and fell into the snow, the son did not even have the energy to reach down or say goodbye.

Kalman could no longer feel his feet, and his mind drifted into a netherworld of sleep, dreams and half-wakefulness; all mingling together to form a bizarre, endless state of limbo - a hallucinatory vision from which there was no escape. His mind could no longer stay awake nor could it fall asleep, so it splintered into separate entities; the motor cortex of his brain controlling the forward locomotion of his legs, stirred on only by the primal instinct of survival, while the higher brain was lost in fleeting, dreamlike visions. To sleep; awake; dream and walk. This is living; dead. The fatigue and cold were so great that only in this manner could he go on. To stop, to think, to question, to feel, meant to die.

They continued on through the night and into the next day, and with each step the hoard of prisoners thinned out as many fell prey to bullets and ice. Kalman maintained his somnambulistic, forward momentum by a sheer will to survive, even though he would have rather died. In a sleeplike vision, he saw his mother sitting by the old wood stove, and he felt for a moment the love she had instilled within him, and this love would not let Kalman's spark of life become extinguished.

By nightfall, the wind and snow had ceased, and a deep, frigid cold settled over the land. Ice crystals hung suspended in the air. As the sun began to set, the sky turned a soft shade of pink. As the horizon darkened, the prisoners were herded into a small sub-camp for the night. The barracks were already filled to capacity and people fought to find a place to sleep or rest. After rummaging through the camp, the only spot Kalman could find was over a latrine. He crawled into a loft space beneath the ceiling and huddled against the corner. He sat suspended between sleep and extreme anxiety when other prisoners began crawling onto the loft. Kalman watched as one person after another clawed their way onto the thin plank. Then, without warning, the supporting two-by-fours began to give way. Kalman struggled to get to his feet as the wood beneath him splintered, sending him plummeting down to the trench below.

In an instant, Kalman was submerged in three feet of human waste. He flung himself out of the trench and ran into an open field, screaming hysterically, covered with excrement, with maggots crawling out of his ears. Crazed and sickened, he hurled himself onto the brittle snow and rolled over and over in an attempt to get the filth off of his body. He brushed wildly at his clothes with his hands and scrubbed at his face and head with snow. He would surely have frozen to death if fellow prisoners hadn't taken pity on him and the others and brought them into the already overflowing barrack. Kalman lay down on the floor, the fetid smell infused into his sinuses, and methodically picked at his skin and clothes in a state of shock.

the dead speak

Before dawn, the exhausted and benumbed prisoners were awakened by angry guards wielding the butts of their rifles and again marched out of camp. Kalman had picked at his skin so much during the night that his arms, legs and chest were bleeding out through his ragged, stained clothes. After walking several kilometers, they came upon a rail yard where the *häftlings* were systematically squeezed into a line of open cattle cars. For the first half an hour it was almost a relief to be crammed inside the car, enveloped by the body heat of closely-packed prisoners and off of the anonymous, endless road they had been on.

Kalman's injured jaw was throbbing so badly he could barely open his mouth, and after an hour and a half he began to wonder how long he could stand as people all around him began buckling onto the hard, metal grating. After eons passed, standing motionless in the cattle car, the cursed train began to move. For several hours it rolled slowly southward into Czechoslovakia; into the mountains and hillside through the bone-chilling coldness. When it came upon a small village the train stopped to refuel and also to let several supply trains pass. What had initially been standing room only thinned out, and the floor was carpeted with human bodies, some barely moving and others stone cold and lifeless.

While Kalman stood against the side of the car, staring blankly at the carnage before him, struggling against hypothermia, hunger and extreme thirst, he heard his name called out.

"Kalman," the voice rang out, softly like an echo. "Karl, is that you?"

The corpses are calling for me. Can it be that the dead speak? Kalman wondered.

Then it came again, a bit more loudly this time. "Karl. Karl. Over here. It's me. Ben"

Kalman slowly looked up, and standing on the other side of the car was his old friend, Ben Fishman.

Kalman stood in disbelief while Ben stepped over the bodies and joined him. They embraced for a moment before Ben spoke. "We have no food but we have to drink."

"But we have no water either," Kalman replied.

"But we have snow."

Kalman looked around the cattle car.

There was no snow. Only bodies and filth.

"Outside, Karl. The ground is covered with snow."

"But we are in here."

"Yes, but when it gets dark, the guards retreat. It's too cold for them to stand outside all night. There's a couple on duty but they can't watch the whole train."

When night fell, the two friends waited until all was clear. When no guards could be seen, Ben slipped over the side of the car and scooped up a pocket of snow with his cap and crawled back into the train with Kalman's help. They ate the snow so quickly to quench their ravishing thirst that the top of their heads felt as though they were being crushed in a vice. After an endless night, the train started moving again. Minutes turned to hours and hours into days as the transport weaved its way through Czechoslovakia like a mouse in a maze, stopping for hours at a time at various stations, the prisoners without food, water or shelter.

Often when passing through the countryside or into a small village, the townspeople cried in disbelief as the doomed train rumbled through, horrified at the sight of such an atrocity. The carriage was strewn with the dead, and Kalman could feel their bones crack beneath his feet. As the train passed underneath a small, arched bridge, he witnessed a group of older women standing on it begin to tear at their hair and scream in disbelief as they watched the train pass. On another occasion, passerby threw rolls and fruit into the car. Kalman reached up to grab an apple and nearly had his hand bit off by other starving prisoners. He never tried again.

Every night Ben and Kalman took turns sneaking off the train to get snow. On the eighth day, Ben had crawled off as usual and was followed by several others who were doing the same. Gunfire rang out. Kalman watched as people were shot off of the side of the train and razed down as they tried to run away. He lost sight of Ben, and when the train departed, he was alone and without his friend. The snow had given many diarrhea, and one night as Kalman lay on top of a body, he felt something warm on his face. The smell then overtook him, and realizing what had just happened, he lashed out at the perpetrator and nearly bit his foot off.

The *häftlings* had been reduced to less than animals, with no understanding, no compassion, no past or future. On the eleventh day, the fetid transport reached its final destination within the Rheinland: Buchenwald.

CHAPTER 15

singing horses and skin

K alman was half asleep and half awake, half alive and half dead, when the cattle cars pulled into Buchenwald. The sky was dark save a few fading stars, stars whose dying light still danced in the evening sky even though their source had burnt out eons ago. Made of the same stardust, humanity was losing its source as well. Quickly dimming, the fading lights within the cattle cars bore witness to the fall.

Flood lights beamed onto the rails as they approached the station. The night air was still brisk, but warmer than it had been in

Auschwitz. As soon as the metal wheels of the train stopped spinning, the gates to the cars were thrust open by the SS.

"Get out! Now! Schnell! Schnell!"

Kalman slowly pulled himself to his feet and stumbled across a pile of corpses while holding onto the side of the carriage for support. Out of 150 people who had loaded onto the car, only 25 got off.

While helping to hold each other up, the remaining 25 prisoners were told to form five columns, the familiar *zu fünf,* and forced to run to a delousing station. Barely able to walk or even stand, Kalman and the others managed to garner the strength to jog into the cold night, pushed on by barking guard dogs, the SS, and sheer will. Kalman managed to stay in the middle of the columns where it was safer and warmer, while the weaker of prisoners were left on the fringes where they were more vulnerable to attack. Once they reached the delousing station, an old, dilapidated barrack, they were made to disrobe and their soiled and tattered rags were burned.

Alone and naked, their bodies and spirits stripped bare, Kalman and the others stood and waited. Hour after hour, as the wind howled and the temperature dropped, Kalman felt himself becoming weaker and weaker. He struggled to stay upright and kept warm by again shifting his weight from one foot to the other. Overcome by thirst, hunger and fatigue, his mind became cloudy and he felt as though he was going to pass out. He shook his head from side to side and inhaled deeply, the infusion of oxygen into his brain keeping him awake and ultimately saving his life.

After seven long hours, those *häftlings* which had survived the night were brought into the delousing station and dusted with caustic powder and then pushed into scolding hot showers. The guards laughed as the prisoners' cold, white skin turned a deep shade of red under the hot steam. Many prisoners passed out from the shock. They were simply pushed aside to make way for the others to continue scrubbing.

After showering, the *häftlings* lined up and were handed clothes; striped pants, a shirt, a cap, shoes, a spoon and a tin bowl. The pants and shirt were two sizes too big, so Kalman rolled up the pant and shirt sleeves before donning the wooden-soled shoes, which were too small and pinched his toes. They were then led to the barracks, and as Kalman hobbled across the grounds with his wooden clogs, he saw a group of prisoners. Four men had been harnessed to a large wagon full of stones. They were being whipped like a pack of mules as they drug the wagon, all the while forced to sing songs for the giggling SS. The look in these "singing horses" faces was one of utter despair, reduced to minstrels in a ghastly vaudevillian act.

Once they had reached the barrack, the door was swung open and the prisoners shoved inside. A foul odor of despair, the air sickly sweet and sticky, overcame them as they entered the unimaginable hovel. Built for 250 prisoners, it now housed over 2000 men. Onto each bunk was stuffed fifteen men, their emaciated bodies squeezed together to form a mass of skin and bones. Each bunk had four planks, making a total of 60 people per bunk.

Kalman sat on the edge of a bunk and dropped his head to his lap. A man sitting next to him was mumbling softly to himself. His skin appeared translucent, revealing the shiny knobs of his knee and elbow joints, his eyes covered with an opaque film.

"Skin," he repeated over and over. "Skin. So much skin."

Kalman tried not to listen to the man, but the man continued rambling on. Suddenly he grabbed Kalman's arm and clenched tightly with his boney fingers.

"Skin. They took tattooed skin and tanned it like cowhide. Stretched out everywhere. And heads. Shrunken heads. Even lampshades made of skin."

The lampshades were for Ilse Koch, the drunken commandant's sadistic wife.

Unable to listen any more, Kalman crawled into the bunk, sandwiched himself between two dying men, and closed his eyes.

the birch tree

After barely being able to sleep, turning from one side to the other in unison as in Auschwitz, the prisoners were awakened before sunrise. They stood in line for over an hour before receiving their one meal for the day, a cup of watery soup and piece of dry bread. Then they were put to work carrying stones. For two weeks Kalman carried the heavy stones back and forth, seemingly without end. Those too weak to handle the work were shot.

At the end of two weeks, Kalman was about to be placed on a work detail building a road from the foot of Ettersberg Mountain to the camp, deemed "Blood Street" by prisoners after thousands had died while working on it, when the Allied bombing again intensified. Weimar, home to Goethe, Bach, Schiller, Wagner, Strauss; Frans Litz, Schopenhauer and Nietzsche, was the closest city to Buchenwald. It was at the foot of the Ettersberg (where Goethe used to sit under a birch tree to work) that the Germans had built Buchenwald, literally, *birch tree*. One can only imagine how these cultural icons would have shuddered in horror at the sight of Hitler's Germany. Even Schopenhauer, the perennial pessimistic philosopher convinced of an indifferent - if not malevolent – universe, and the inherent meaningless of life, could have never imagined such evil; nor could Nietzsche grasp the bastardization of his *Will to Power*.

Now Weimar, the historic cultural capitol of Germany, was burning and the black smoke could be seen from Buchenwald. Kalman, being experienced in defusing unexploded bombs, was chosen with a group of others to go into Weimar and search for the ticking time bombs. The prisoners were forbidden to walk on the sidewalks and had to take their caps off whenever a uniformed soldier passed. In between his labors of digging up and snipping bombs, Kalman risked his life many times picking up rotten apples or peanuts out of the gutter. Anything to chew on would suffice.

Though some of the civilians acted as if the *häftlings* were invisible, others dropped fruit or bread onto the road for the prisoners to eat. One elderly woman with soft, white, hair and a slight crook in her back, filled a bag full of rolls and pierced a hole in the bottom of it. She strolled down the street near the haggard prisoners and the rolls started dropping from the bag. Understanding full well that if caught, she would be hung herself, she continued walking until all of the rolls had dropped from the sack. The prisoners scrambled to the bread like starving dogs, the promise of food more powerful than any bullet could have ever been.

white sheets and purple cabbage

Those who didn't die from exhaustion or starvation were often subject to medical experiments, shot or tortured to death, while ones like Kalman, who were still of some use to the Nazi's, went on as best they could. The barracks started to thin out, making more room for the survivors on the bunks. This was of small consolation to the pitiful *häftlings* of Buchenwald.

Kalman had grown numb to the fact that he could be blown into tiny specks of flesh every time he defused a bomb, it would be quick and painless, and many days he hoped that he would be. While reaching for a wire one overcast afternoon, warplanes began flying overhead. Sirens sounded and everyone ran off the streets, including the soldiers. As the bombs started to fall, Kalman ran into a vacant house to seek shelter. He hid in a bedroom, and there before him was a bed with clean, crisp, white sheets and pillowcases. He stood and stared at the white sheets in disbelief. It had been nearly *six years* since he had seen such a thing, and had forgotten what a clean bed and white sheets even looked like.

After the bombing stopped, Kalman contemplated for a moment whether to stay in the house, but knowing that if he was caught, he would be shot on the spot, he went back outside and joined the other prisoners before the guards came out. They were immediately put to work again and Kalman went about unearthing a bomb from the dirt. He had dug half way down when he hit something soft and moist. He cleared away the remaining soil and exposed a patch of purple cabbage. Though it was writhing with worms, Kalman stuffed his pants and shirt full of 10 kilos of cabbage and managed to smuggle it back to camp. That night, the prisoners in his barrack feasted on purple cabbage. A gift from the earth itself.

CHAPTER 16

one minute at a time

In February of 1945, a garrison of SS soldiers accompanied by a camp doctor and several officers scoured Buchenwald for five hundred of the youngest and healthiest men and boys for a special selection. The physician, whose job it was to perform horrific medical experiments on live prisoners, stopped briefly in front of Kalman, looked him up and down and said; "He will do."

To receive a verdict from such a man was a death sentence. Kalman only hoped it would be quick and painless, but rather than being led to the 'clinic', he was placed in formation with the other *chosen ones*, given bread and water and marched a few kilometers, where they were then herded into a line of closed cattle cars, roughly sixty people per car.

Kalman lay in the darkness and listened to the rumbling of the wheels as the train proceeded toward an unknown destination. The further the train traveled, the colder it became, until the railcar felt like a meat locker. After three days and three nights, the train came to a stop. When the car door was opened, a solid sheet of ice covered the entrance-way like a plate of frozen glass, formed from the breath of prisoners. The icy shield was shattered by the fury of rifle butts, sending sharp fragments of *breath* onto the *häftlings* before they were drug out by the SS and taken to an unfinished, two-story brick barrack.

For the remainder of the day and throughout the night they stayed in the barren barracks, lost and forgotten. Joe Kahn and his brother Henry, friends of Kalman who were also on the transport, found Kalman sitting next to a pile of broken bricks.

"Karl! You're alive!"

Kalman looked up to find two old friends standing before him.

"Joe? Henry? Is that really you?"

"What's left of us," Joe answered, lifting his shirt to expose his bony ribs. "And it ain't much."

Kalman smiled briefly, then patting his own stomach, said; "I'd give you some of mine but I'm afraid there's nothing there."

The two brothers plopped down next to Kalman. "Where are we Karl?"

"I don't know."

"Is this a hospital? I was sure we were going with the doctor."

"Me too. If it is we're as good as dead."

"Or better off dead," Henry interjected. "The things I hear those doctors are doing with people you'd rather be dead."

"I don't think so," Kalman went on. "This don't look like no hospital. Nope, it isn't no hospital."

The following day the *häftlings* were taken from the barrack and led outside to a small field where they were introduced to the camp commandant, a middle-aged, weasely fellow known for his cruelty. He resembled a possum, with a long, pointy nose and stubble jutting out from beneath his lower lip like misplaced whiskers. His eyes were a pale brownish color and were always darting back and forth nervously. When he smiled his mouth contorted into a hideous grin.

The commandant looked over the prisoners and then informed them that they were chosen as laborers and that their lives depended on their ability to work. The prisoners later learned that an armament factory was being built nearby.

"Look around people, this is your new home," the commandant began.

The camp itself was very small, the only substantial building being the brick barracks. There were no barbed-wire fences or guard towers, although there were plenty of SS soldiers milling about.

"Escape is futile," the possum continued. "Don't let the open fields fool you. Look around closely."

To one side was a wide, fast-moving river; to the other a mountainous range capped with snow.

"There is nowhere to go. If you don't drown in the river or freeze in the mountains, you will be hung."

The prisoners were then divided up into groups of fifty, fed a small piece of dry bread, a cup of grass soup and immediately set to work. Kalman and the Kahn brothers were put to work pushing huge, cement pipes. It took ten men over an hour to roll the pipe less than one hundred meters. Guards stood by and whipped anyone they felt didn't sufficiently put their backs into it. The hard labor continued well into the night until the men were completely exhausted and could barely stand.

That night while lying in the barrack, Henry Kahn told Kalman, "I can't do it. I can't go on like this. I felt my back beginning to break. I'm so tired."

"Just keep going," Kalman told him. "Don't think about it. Put your mind somewhere else. Just do it one minute at a time."

By the time Kalman had finished his sentence, Henry was asleep.

digesting oneself

Meals were served three times a day, the same bread and grassy soup, which didn't provide enough fuel for even one hour's work, let alone to sustain twelve to thirteen hours of hard labor, day in and day out. There was no kitchen in the camp, so a group of prisoners were sent into the nearby village of Speichingen each day to carry back large pots of the green, watery liquid on wooden poles. Speichingen was a small German village near the Swiss border. To the villagers of Speichingen, the prisoners were nothing more than transparent ghosts.

Kalman was pulled from the Kahn's work detail and put into a shaft where his job was to pat down the concrete as it was being poured into the hole. After several days of this, his back was so stiff that he couldn't straighten up without burning pain shooting across his lower back and down his legs. There was no laundry or change of clothes, and after a couple of weeks, Kalman's shirt and pants became so stiff with cement dust that they could stand better than he could. His hunger became so great that he began eating dead birds, roots, rotten potatoes and bugs. After nearly six years under the Nazi rule, it was at Speichingen that Kalman felt himself becoming a *musselmann*. His emaciated body started devouring itself, absorbing what little fat and muscle it had left and turning it into fuel. The pain of digesting oneself, of slowly starving to death, was excruciating and without end.

Lethargic of body and mind, Kalman sat with Joe Kahn for a paltry morning meal. Several young *häftlings* had attempted to escape three days earlier and their bloated corpses were hanging from poles on a nearby hill. Henry Kahn was absent and Kalman assumed he had been devoured by death as well; for it was death that was the true king of the fields. His mind was cloudy from lack of food, and even death could not stir him from his deep apathy. What little emotion he had remaining spun through his body like a drunken roller-coaster. Escape from Speichingen was futile, but escape from one's own body and mind bore even greater futility. To survive one more day was the only choice, but the choice itself seemed futile. To survive an existence which was not even existence meant nothing. But the tiny spark of life, the flame within the hurricane, still would not be extinguished.

"Henry is not well," Joe Kahn told Kalman quietly. "He could not get up this morning."

Kalman felt a deep pang of sadness in his gut. "Perhaps he just needs to rest," he told his friend, who was very pale himself and wheezed when he talked, with beads of perspiration streaming down his face, even in the cold winter air.

"Um-hmm," Joe mumbled as he stared off into the distance. "I wish I was sitting on top of that mountain. I would lie down and sleep forever, like Rip Van Winkle," he went on.

Rip Van Winkle? A book? Kalman had forgotten that books even existed. Books belonged to humanity. Humanity was gone.

"Stand up!" Guards began to yell. "Do you think you're on vacation? There is work to be done! *Schnell! Schnell!*"

Kalman slowly rose to his feet and helped his friend to stand up, who was now coughing violently. "Come Joe, we must go now."

Each tablespoon of cement felt as if it weighed a ton, and tons of it was poured into the shaft - poured down to Kalman where he struggled to keep up the impossible pace. His right foot began to itch and then to burn. At the end of the day while returning to the barrack, he had developed a painful limp. Once inside the barrack, he wrestled the clog off his swollen foot, which was caked with cement, and promptly fell asleep.

When Kalman woke up the next day, his foot was on fire. The cement had flaked off his skin during the night, exposing a foot three times its normal size, blazing red and purulent. Even to breathe sent searing pain up his leg, so Kalman lie still and struggled not to move. The barracks emptied out as the others were sent back to work, while the sick and dying were left to themselves.

Among them were Kalman, the Kahn brothers, and roughly thirty others.

Each hour the foot grew larger, until the skin was pulled tightly across the bones like a drum; red and shiny with deep, crimson veins pounding with every heartbeat. By evening the swelling and redness had begun to travel up the leg. The following morning Kalman was burning with fever and a deep, purple track reached from his ankle to his knee like a grotesque spider's web. With no water to drink, his parched lips turned white and cracked, while the poison in his blood condensed into a septic sludge.

On the third day the pain was unbearable. Unable to get out of the bunk or even wiggle his toes, Kalman waited to die. Joe Kahn was lying in a bunk nearby, struggling to breathe, while Henry already looked like a corpse, when the doors to the barrack swung open and several SS guards entered the building.

"Looks like you're all going for a ride," one of the guards announced. "The commandant wants you to visit the mountains and get some fresh air."

"Everyone must get out. Hurry!" They insisted.

Those who could walk disembarked, while the weaker ones stayed put.

Kalman was the last to be gathered up, and when they grabbed him off of the bunk, he nearly passed out from the searing pain. They were placed in the back of a truck and driven a short distance to the mountains. Kalman was relieved that the pain would soon be over. At last death would liberate him. When the truck reached a narrow pass, it came to stop and the driver and two guards got out of the cab. Kalman could hear them talking outside for a moment, and then they came around to the back of the truck.

The guards had been ordered to take the *häftlings* out and shoot them, but when they reached the mountains, they discovered a line of cattle cars full of prisoners idling on the tracks and decided to put their sick passengers onto the train.

One by one, the weak prisoners were carried to the cattle cars by the three soldiers. When they reached Kalman, one guard took him by the hands while the other grabbed his feet. Kalman screamed hysterically; "My foot! My foot! Please don't touch my foot!" The excruciating pain shot through his body like a lighting bolt. He continued screaming as the guards carried him to the cattle car. "Be quiet!" a guard shouted. "We're trying to help you, can't you see that!"

"My foot! Oh God my foot!" he continued yelling as the guards swung him back and forth, and on count of three tossed him into the carriage like a sack of flour.

breath and bread

Kalman crumpled onto a pile of dead and dying prisoners in the middle of the railcar, screaming wildly; "My foot, don't kick my foot," while trying desperately to show them his infected leg. He then pulled himself into the corner of the car and sat between two other young, emaciated *häftlings*. The man to the right was a few years older than Kalman. "Looks bad," he said feebly, referring to Kalman's foot.

"It hurts. It hurts so bad," Kalman cried.

The boy to the left couldn't have been any older than fifteen. His eyes were cloudy and his breathing was rapid and shallow. He stared vacantly into the car, looking but not seeing, and was drifting rapidly into another place. In his left hand he held a piece of uneaten bread. Kalman and the other prisoner stared at the bread and desperately wanted to grab it to feed their starving bodies. But the boy clenched the bread tightly in his fist, holding on with every last ounce of strength he had left. The only way to pry it loose would be to kill him. Though Kalman had been reduced to less than an animal, he was no murderer.

So they waited, Kalman and the man to his right , for the boy to die. He lasted through the night. When the morning sun broke its way through the vent on top of the car, sending rays of sunshine through the musty air, the boy let out his last breath; a final gasp of air followed by a slow whooshing sound, the low hum of death; and the bread dropped from his hand. Kalman slowly reached over and picked up the bread from the boy's lap and he and his fellow prisoner shared in its nourishment. Through the boy's death, Kalman and the other man were given a small piece of life.

end of the line

Thirty-six ticks to the chime brought the transport into the heart of Germany, near Munich, to the first concentration camp ever built by Hitler and his henchmen. *Dachau.*

It arrived like all other trains had arrived, to madness and mayhem.

Coming to a halt just outside of the camp, the prisoners were taken out of the cars and placed in a line to be processed and registered. Kalman, being unable to walk or even to stand, stayed behind. This was the end of the line. There was nowhere to run even if he could run. There was no water. No food. No sanitation.

Just the agonizing pain in his foot and the bodies of those who had died on the trip. Kalman expected to soon join them. He shut his eyes and leaned onto the metal trellis of the car. Too sick and too tired to struggle any longer, his expressionless face frozen in limbo, he sat and waited.

As he began to drift off, he heard voices outside of the car. He braced himself for the inevitable. He did not open his eyes. He did not want to see the faces of his executioners. The clang of shoes stepping onto the steel floor reverberated through the car. Kalman held his breath. His body stiffened. Then the voices came.

"Hey you! You can't stay in here. You'll die."

But these weren't the voices of guards. They spoke Yiddish. Not German. Kalman opened his eyes and standing before him was several prisoners, led by the man he had shared bread with.

"Come on boy, we have to get you out of here."

Before he could begin to comprehend what was happening, the prisoners were by his side.

"Watch his foot," his old companion warned the others. "He can't take much more." Then they scooped him up and carried him outside where they had a wheelbarrow waiting. They placed him in the wheelbarrow and rolled him to the gate to be registered.

The guard at the gate looked at Kalman sitting in the wheelbarrow. The others stood by nervously, hoping he wouldn't be taken away or that they would all be shot.

"What's wrong with him?" the SS soldier asked.

"It's his foot, sir. He can't walk."

The inane guard paused for a moment.

"Jew or Pole," he asked.

Kalman, feeling a slight glimmer of hope, responded quickly in perfect Polish;

"Polish, sir, I'm a Pole."

"Take him," the guard ordered the others. "Get him out of my sight, the smell of his foot is making me sick."

As his companions were about to grab the handles of the wheelbarrow, the guard yelled out again; "Take him to the Polish infirmary, maybe they can cut that stinking thing off."

The infirmary was nothing but an old barrack full of bunks. There was no medicine. No doctors. No nurses. Kalman was given a gown and an old blanket. For the first two days he lay in his cot, unable to even get up to relieve himself. A man next to him had died days earlier and the body was beginning to decompose. Kalman yelled and yelled about the smell, until at last the corpse was taken away. On the third day he woke up to a miracle. The infection in his leg had begun to recede. He had watched the guards deliver meals to bunks assigned to various prisoners, and when the bunks had been unknowingly vacated, he struggled to his feet and hobbled over to them to get extra food. He was always careful to keep covered by the gown so as not to expose his circumcised penis. When he urinated into a pale he would first retire to a corner.

Kalman felt himself slowly getting stronger until one day the infection returned. Burning with fever, his body covered in cold sweat, he became weaker and weaker. He could no longer get off the bunk. He did not eat. He could not drink. Bodies were being carried out of the barracks daily. His was sure to be next.

He lie naked on a bed of moldy straw and covered himself with a tattered blanket. For the first time in six years he prayed. The prayer is simple and direct. He asked only that he may die.

"Please God, let me die. Let me die. Please, just let me die."

The flame of his spirit was the flicker of a candle against a hurricane. It had kept burning for six years– but it could burn no more. As the prayerful words began to die out, muffled between the blanket and straw, a disheveled man burst in through the door of the barrack. Running up to the man lying in the bunk next to Kalman, he began yelling excitedly. "Hold on brother! Please hold on! They're coming! The Americans are coming. You can hear their guns. Please hold on – they're sure to be here in five or six hours. Just hold on a little longer," he pleaded desperately.

"Six hours," the young man's voice rang out.

Kalman could not register the sound or the voice; he could not have repeated what he had just heard, but deep within his mind, he knew – and he understood. **"They're coming…six hours…."**

Kalman began to silently count, slowly and deliberately, without thought. "Six years. Six months, Six weeks. Six Days. Six hours." And faded into a dream….

……he slowly opened his eyes. All was white. The place he now lay was pure white and his skin was cocooned in softness…………

EPILOGUE

The dawn of a new day. The dawn of a new life. But what of life? All that Kalman had known was gone. His family, over seventy members in all, gone. His mother and father; grandparents, brothers and sisters, all had been devoured by the beast. His past, his childhood, his culture. All vanished. Who had lost more, those who had perished, or those who had survived?

Berlin, Dresden, and many other cities and villages throughout Europe were in ruins. Nagasaki and Hiroshima lie smoldering under a radioactive sky, while the world celebrated the war's end and began to rebuild. Parisians cried with joy along the *Champs-Élysées.* New Yorkers danced, hugged and kissed in Times Square. Farmers in Nebraska and miners in Wyoming;

factory workers in Liverpool and fishermen in Wales, welcomed their sons and daughters back and mourned those who did not. The Belgian and Dutch rose out from under the weight of the occupation to begin anew, while Stalin clamped his murderous vice onto Russia and Eastern Europe.

The camps were empty. The ovens cold. The demonic duo, Hitler and Himmler, dead by their own hands. The worst mankind had to offer – cowardice to the end. Alfred Mädel, the sadistic kapo, was said to have beaten to death by former prisoners. The Third Reich had been destroyed. But the memories remained. The pain of deep loss ever present. Even guilt for having survived at all. There was no going back. No reclaiming the past. There was only one day. This day. This one day to be lived, minute by minute, onward towards an uncertain future.

Kalman lay in a coma for three weeks after being found in a crematorium atop a pile of corpses. He was nothing but skin on bone. After several more weeks in the hospital, he slowly regained some weight and the infection in his leg healed. He was given a pair of underwear, the first underwear he had seen in six years, a shirt and pair of pants from an old Panzer uniform, a pair of shoes and then released from the hospital in Munich. From there he went to a Displaced Persons camp outside of the city. The rooms were fairly comfortable, and while eating chicken and meatballs, Kalman felt himself slowly being delivered out of hell.

On a warm, beautiful day in May, he decided to lie out and get some sun. He took a tube of what he thought was sunscreen and slabbed it all over his body. It turned out to be toothpaste, which dried and caked onto his skin. Realizing his mistake, he laughed.

He laughed for the first time in many years. He had no money, no trade, and nowhere to call home, but he could still laugh.

Four months later, his brother Charley, who was living in a DP camp in Landsberg am Lech, found Kalman's name on a survivors list. He and three other friends, including their old companion Ignat Stieglitz from Dombrowa, hopped on a train and traveled to Munich to reunite with Carl.

Kalman assumed his younger brother had been killed with all the rest, and when he saw Charley walk into the room that one, rainy afternoon, he was overcome with joy. His brother and best friend was alive! A miracle upon miracles!

Chiel, or Charles as he was known in America, had survived several labor camps himself, including the infamous labor camp at Plaszow where they were forced to exhume an estimated 8000 corpses from mass graves and burn them as depicted in the film "Schindler's List." Charles remembered unearthing mothers who were still holding onto their children. Unable to face the horror any longer, Charles and one fellow prisoner decided not to go to work one day, even if it meant being shot. As it turned out, everyone in their work detail was killed that day. Charles and the other prisoner were spared and shipped to another labor camp, and one week later, as luck or fate would have it, he was sent to the town of Bruunlitz in the Sudentenland where he ended up being prisoner # 377 on Schindler's list under the name Chiel Kohane. There he remained, housed and fed, until liberation. His greatest blow came when he returned to Dombrowa to find his family gone.

"What reason do I have to be alive?" he wondered.

The first reason, and his greatest joy, came upon finding his older brother still alive.

For several months they lived at the DP camp in Landsberg am Lech, and finally found an apartment in Munich. The injury to Kalman's jaw became malignant and he suffered eight operations and six months in the hospital before it was finally managed successfully with the first Radium machine ever used in Germany.

They picked up odd jobs, bought food on the black market, and skirted the police who were always looking for vagrant criminals. Charley was accused of stealing and faced two years in jail, but Kalman convinced a doctor to tell the police that Charley was insane and must be let go. Charley was released and perfectly sane.

The two brothers wanted to immigrate to Israel, but Israel would not take Kalman right away because of his injury. "There's a war going on here, you'd die in the gutter," they told him. "Wait a couple of years and then come." So the two brothers decided to immigrate to America. They had two aunts living in New Jersey, so Kalman packed up his valise, procured the papers, and sailed across the sea, arriving in Boston with two dollars in his pocket and a foreign tongue. "I thought America was paved with gold," Kalman reflected. "Instead I saw men digging trenches on the street on a Sunday for a few pennies a day."

He took a train to New York and was met by his uncle and two aunts who then drove him to Jersey City. When Kalman entered the lobby to their apartment building, he thought, "My God, look at this room, it's true, in America they live like kings." Then while taking the elevator up, he observed, "They even have their own private elevator." Once out of the elevator they proceeded down the hallway and entered the apartment, a small, one bedroom, with two aunts, an uncle and now Karl living in it. "So much for the mansion," Karl laughed.

His uncle brought him to a barber for a haircut, bought him a suit and new shoes, and helped to find him a job. One day Kalman told his aunt what had happened to grandmother and the aunt began crying hysterically. His uncle took Kalman aside and told him, "Karl, you must forget what happened. You cannot bring them back. You're in America now. You must start a new life. Talking about it won't change it."

And for twenty years Kalman never did. He reunited with Ben Fishman and the Kahn brothers who had also survived. He married a wonderful woman, had a son and daughter, and built a successful and well known delicatessen in Philadelphia by the name of Hymie's Deli with his brother Charley. After twenty years in the deli business, he sold the company and became a successful stock broker until retiring in South Palm Beach, Florida.

In 1968 he visited Israel. He stood before the Wailing Wall and cried. Through his tears, Grandfather Kohane appeared before him, and Kalman remembered his beloved grandfather's dying words. "Someone must live to tell the story." At that moment Kalman vowed to tell the story to anyone who would listen; that the world must not forget. After hearing someone say the Holocaust was a hoax, he was more determined than ever. He began speaking at Synagogues, churches, schools, and to this day, he continues to do so. He could never forget, and has said many times, "It is unbelievable even for me, and I was there."

His son Hal is a successful music producer in New York and the Musical Producer for Saturday Night Live. His daughter is happily married and has two children of her own.

But what of Kalman? Who is he? Who is the man beyond the success and achievement? Kalman Willner, whose name was changed to Carl in America, is the man who told me the first time I met him, standing in his living room in his eighth floor apartment overlooking the ocean; "Never take anything for granted."

He is a man with great humor and wit. A glint in his eyes and a quick smile. Honest and forthright, he puts on no pretense. What you see is what you get. He is a man who loves to dance, who acted in three plays and was chosen MVP by his fellow actors. "They kept calling me a ham," he laughed. "Why would they call me a pig?" He had wondered, until his wife, after she had stopped laughing, told him it was a compliment. A man, who, when meeting Bono of the band U2, a friend of his son, while everyone was racing to the door to meet the famous musician, had only one thing to say. "These peanuts are too spicy."

He is a man who went on to live a happy and joyous life, even though the memories would always haunt him. He is the essence of a person whose spirit faced the greatest evil mankind has ever known – and triumphed!

And as for Charles? After joining Carl in America, he helped build Hymie's into a burgeoning business. He was happily married and had three children and eight wonderful grandchildren. After selling Hymies in 1976, he went on to establish a successful commercial real estate business in Philadelphia, and was blessed with many friends

Age plus the years spent doing hard labor took a toll on Charles' body. His back and shoulders began to stoop, yet his face remained full, his brilliant, blue eyes alive with gentle wisdom and a spry intellect. When asked once how he would like to be remembered, he stated simply, "That I was a nice man." He was grateful for having survived to the end of his days. Though faced with bitter cruelty, Carl and Charles remained kind and caring men, and throughout their lives, the brothers Willner remained steadfast in their belief in themselves and in each person's inherent worth as human beings.

Their souls had survived…and soared.

The humble human spirit, wonderfully resilient, remains strong.

~

THE END

About the author;
Von Petersen was born in the high desert hills of Rock Springs, Wyoming, in the heart of the Rocky Mountains. Catching a ride on the leaves of sagebrush as a teenager, he has since lived throughout the United States and in Antwerp, Belgium. Serpentine paths are sometimes difficult to navigate, but provide abundant fodder for a curious life. He would like to thank all those who have shared their own paths with him along the way. His daughter is the artist, Centa Petersen.

VON AND CARL
SOUTH PALM BEACH, FL
2006

Printed in the United States
143475LV00013B/78/P

9 781435 709386